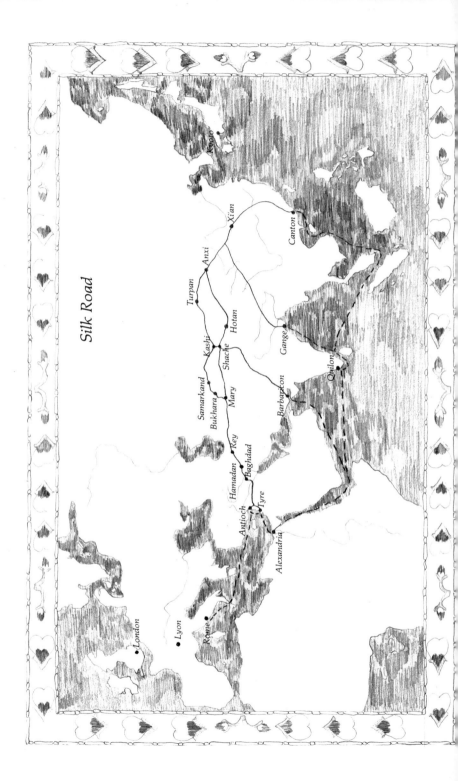

A
SILK WORKER'S NOTEBOOK

Cheryl Kolander

illustrations by Ann Sabin

INTERWEAVE PRESS, INC.
306 North Washington Avenue
Loveland, Colorado 80537

Library of Congress Catalog Number 85-080616
ISBN 0-934026-18-1

ACKNOWLEDGEMENTS

Especial thanks to the following, who have helped and encouraged this work:

John Bauguess
Anne Bliss
Deborah Dant
Mary DeBone
Susan Druding
Bette and Bernard Hochberg
Susan Goldin
Susan Gowey
Linda Ligon
R. McCreary
Doris and George Maslach

Jean and Roger Moss
Rocky Stone & Family,
    M&M Printers
Barbara Nordin
Marc M. Owens
Irene and Lisa Zenev
R. Zappa, Gamage Cup Books
    and all who have con-
    tributed photos and shared
    their experience of working
    with silk.

Miscellaneous illustrations

page 7. *Flowering vine.* Embroidery. Japan. Drawn from a Japanese book on design: 日本の女の装

page 95. *Chrysanthemum.* Embroidery. Japan. Drawn from the same source as the above.

page 153. *Goose.* Brocade. Italy. 14th century. Drawn from Flemming, Plate 57.

CONTENTS

Gor ("The Wild Ass"). Syrian or Byzantine samite, after a Persian design. Seventh-8th century. The horseman is Sassanian King Bahram V Gor (A.D. 420-438) who, with a single arrow, shot both a wild ass and an attacking leopard through their hearts, a legendary feat. Red, gold and light green, on a dark green ground. Flemming, Plate 17, and Volbach, Plate 46. Present location: the Church of Sant'Ambrogio, Milan, where it is used to cover the inner faces of the doors of the gold altar.

Chapter 1
HISTORY

he history of silk begins in China. Writing in
A.D. 90 Ssŭ-ma Ch'ién tells the story of Si-
ling, wife of the fabled "Yellow Emperor",
Huang-ti. One day, it is said, she dropped a
cocoon into her tea. It began to unravel.
This gave her the idea of unreeling the cocoons into long floating threads of silk.

Silk was probably in use in China long before this,
though, as the symbol of *ssŭ*, silk, was already a part of the
written language at the time of Huang-ti and Si-ling, ca. 2600
B.C.

Although the cultivation of silk began in China, and fragments of Chinese silks as old as 1500 B.C. have been found, the
oldest written record of the fiber's use comes from India. The
Ramayana and the *Mahabharata* speak of the weaving of silks.
These Sanskrit epics are sacred texts of the Aryans who, in the
middle of the second millenium B.C., swept down from the

northern plains and eventually established an empire from India west to the Mediterranean. The introduction of the horse to Europe and to Egypt is attributed to them, and it is likely that silks came, too.

Aristotle, about 300 B.C., gives the first mention in western literature of the source of silk: a "curious horned worm". How common the fiber was then is not clear; it was little mentioned by the ancient Greeks. Perhaps silk was known, but despised, as a symbol of the hated Persians. Aristotle's passage attributes the first weaving of silk to Pamphile, a Phoenician princess on the island of Cos, off Turkey. The fabric, of great renown, was described as "woven wind". Aristotle describes the silkworm, but whether Pamphile cultivated silk is disputed. If she did, the knowledge was soon lost; later writers didn't even credit Aristotle, and give all sorts of odd stories about the source of silk.

Meanwhile, in China, silk had become so abundant that by the Han dynasty, ca. 200 B.C. to A.D. 200, silk fabric was part of a soldier's wages. China can be likened to a beautiful valley, surrounded on all sides by natural barriers: high mountains, cold wastes inhabited by "Barbarian" nomads, and the vast sea to the east. Little is known about the time much before the Han, in terms of trade beyond the frontiers, for all the Chinese history books were burned in 212 B.C. We do know the situation at the beginning of the Han was one of externally enforced isolation. Fear of the Nomads who inhabited the mountains and deserts to the north and west kept the Chinese within their "beautiful valley". But internal peace allowed a great production of goods. A far-sighted emperor charged his General Chang K'ien to attempt a passage across the desert, in hopes of establishing friendly trading relations with the peoples to the west. Others had gone before, but Chang K'ien was the first to return. The round trip took 20 years.

Soon after, under Wu-ti (140-86 B.C.), the Western Barbarians were subdued, and regular trade routes were established across the desert. Garrisons protected the route just as forts protected the wagon trails across the plains and deserts of North America in the 1800s.

The establishment of this **Silk Road** marks the beginning of abundant silk in the West.

In Rome, wealthy women unraveled the heavy Chinese

The cultivated, white silk-producing caterpillar of China had been introduced into India sometime before 200 A.D.

It is said a Chinese princess, married off to a distant and foreign king, smuggled out the eggs in her headdress.

Did she want to continue her sericulture and weaving, preferred pastimes of Chinese noble women?

Or did she shrewdly plan to bring a dowry so valuable that she could never be slighted?

India has many species of native wild silkworms. But the delicacy, the shimmering whiteness, of the mulberry silk has always been admired.

designs and rewove them into revealing gauzes, or into tapestries, a few of which have survived. At Palmyra, a western focus of the southern trade routes which were partly by sea, Chinese fabrics of about A.D. 200 have been unearthed. Many fragments and sizable pieces of silks dating from the Han and following T'ang have been found along the area of the desert overland routes. Many fabrics have also been found in graves of nomadic chieftains who raided the caravans. (Not only Chinese silks going west, but also Persian and Greco-Roman fabrics which had been going east.) These Han silks are of impressive workmanship. They are elaborate in technique and use exceedingly fine threads, with colors still well preserved. Designs range from phantasmagoric swirling clouds to bold but charming stylized animals and flowers. Some recently unearthed embroideries of probably earlier date are in designs of cloud swirls done on open mesh, pattern-woven gauze.

The Persians quickly established themselves as the sole middlemen between East and West in the silk trade. Then war broke out between Byzantium and Persia in the 500s, and the West was cut off from its supply. The Emperor Justinian recognized what the Chinese had known for millenia and what many later kings would also recognize: produce silk, and you have an inexhaustible gold mine.

The story goes that two Nestorian monks who had been living in China offered to return there and smuggle out the starts of sericulture: silkworm eggs and white mulberry seeds. Their journey is said to have taken only two years, a remarkably short time, and some authorities believe they actually went to North India rather than China. When the monks returned to Constantinople, they were housed on the palace grounds and given everything they could use to successfully begin sericulture in the West. Of course, it went slowly at first, and the whole enterprise did nothing to relieve the current shortage of silk. But the eventual results are impressive: all the races of European silkworms up through the 1700s descended from those first eggs.

The Arabs were the real spreaders of silk in the Mediterranean. From its establishment in Turkey and Greece they carried it to Sicily, and across North Africa, and into Spain. Silk culture went hand in hand with silk weaving, and some fragments of beautiful arabesqued brocades survive from this Mediterranean period.

Northern Europe was in the Dark Ages. Only the nobility could afford the rich and costly imported silks. But the Crusades changed this. Rich and poor alike went off to fight the Arabs; rich and poor alike saw and brought home fine satins, damasks and brocades. Many of these were given to churches where everyone could see them and marvel at their beauty.

Silk culture and weaving traveled up the boot of Italy, and flourished in the climate of the North. Venice, Lucca, Florence became renowned centers of silk weaving from the 14th century, specializing in heavy brocades and patterned velvets. Silks were exported to the whole of northern Europe and the wealth garnered from the silk trade is credited as one of the financial bases of the Renaissance. The Piedmont region of Italy continued to produce some of the finest raw silk in the world (many say the finest) until about the beginning of this century.

The Confucian history, the *Shu Ching*, lists silk fabrics as one of the tributes exacted by central China from neighboring regions under the reign of the Great Yu, 2205-2197 B.C.

The *Shu Ching*, written about 500 B.C. is one of the few ancient histories to have escaped the burning of the books. It was based on documents ancient at the time.

Chronic political troubles led some silk weavers to flee Italy for France. Efforts were made by several French kings to encourage this resettlement. Louis XI granted emigré silk weavers complete exemption from taxes. To solve a shortage of raw silk, mulberry trees were planted by royal decree, including some in the Tuilleries (still standing, I believe). Colbert, the far-sighted agricultural minister to Louis XIV, helped organize the weavers and the trade in order to improve the quality of the finished silks. France, especially the area around Lyons, soon became the center of European silk weaving. Technical improvements to the silk-weaving drawloom resulted, under the reign of Louis XVI, in the elaborate naturalistic brocades of Philippe de LaSalle.

Monarchs of other countries attempted to establish, or widen, the area of sericulture in their realms. The New World colonies were strongly encouraged in it. Spain established sericulture in Mexico, but it declined after royal patronage ceased. Today, though, wild silk is gathered in at least one area. In the mountains outside Oaxaca, native Zapotecans gather a very fine, light-shaded wild silk off oak trees and hand spin and weave it into a thin crêpe. It is then dyed bright magenta and used for a wrap-around belt. Possibly, this use of wild silk predates the Spanish.

King James I heavily encouraged silk raising in the North American colonies of England. He saw it as an alternative to the lucrative tobacco which was rapidly supplanting every other crop. James was violently opposed to smoking, considering it an ungodly habit.

Sericulture in England never was commercially successful because of the cool, damp climate. But several regions in England are renowned for their fine silk weaving. These centers were established by Flemish and French weavers fleeing religious persecution on the Continent, in the period 1585-1685. Macclesfield and Spitalfields became major centers, and Macclesfield continues to produce fine-woven silks.

In the United States

Silk raising has never been commercially successful in the U.S. either, although the climate is excellent. The high cost of labor is a major reason. Silk growing was encouraged by the colonial governments, but tobacco and then cotton were more profitable. However, silk raising was carried on in many households, including those of a governor of Connecticut and a president of Yale. Franklin had started a communal filature — silk reeling house — in Philadelphia, before the war interrupted.

In the 1830s there was a spectacular boom and bust centering on a new type of mulberry, the *Morus multicaulis*. It was touted as a more freely growing food for the silkworms. It turned out to be unpalatable, as well as frost tender, and the boom busted after a few years. A blight attacked the remaining mulberry trees in 1844 and destroyed what silk raising as was still going on, principally in Connecticut. But by the 1920s a remarkable amount of silk was being raised on the West Coast, especially around San Diego. The cocoons were sent to Japan for reeling.

While high-hoped attempts at raising silk on a commercial scale generally failed, the manufacture of silk, from raw-reeled to finished thread and silk goods, attained large proportions. These processes were easily mechanized, and, before synthetics took the place of silk in the popular market, the U.S. was probably the largest manufacturer of silk goods in the world. Many of the huge brick factory buildings are still standing, and are used for related goods. The Belding Heminway, Carlson-Currier silk works at Petaluma, California, is now Sunset Line & Twine, linen and fish line twisters. If the "Belding" sounds familiar, it should! Belding-Corticelli silk sewing thread and buttonhole twist were in nearly every fabric shop until very recently.

In Japan

On the other side of China, silk flowered in ancient Japan. Japanese chronicles relate that a Chinese emperor around A.D. 200 exchanged gifts with envoys from Japan. The more treasured of the gifts: silkworm eggs. (And this at a time when sericulture was still a secret closely guarded from the West.) Soon after, an exiled Chinese prince, his household, and all his followers' households fled to Japan. There they took up silk weaving as their livelihood, transplanting the skills of China to the cultivated and fertile soil of the small island nation.

For several centuries silk weaving in Japan paralleled that in China. But eventually China was subject to European influence, and her fabric styles changed. Japan, though, maintained

The earliest allusions to silk in western literature seem to be two references in the *Old Testament*: Ezekiel xvi, 10, 13; *meshi*, silken gauze:

10   I clothed thee also with broidered work, and shod thee with badgers' skin, and I girdled thee about with fine linen, and I covered thee with silk.

13   Thus wast thou decked with gold and silver; and thy rainment was of fine linen and silk, and broidered work; thou didst eat fine flour, and honey, and oil: and thou wast exceeding beautiful, and thou didst prosper into a kingdom.

"A cultured Japanese considers few treasures more to be cherished than a piece of rare old patterned silk of the type we call brocade. Intrinsically such a possession frequently rivals gold or precious stones in value, and its sentimental worth is often greater. Jewels have been seldom worn by the Japanese until very recent times, and gold and silver have traditionally been regarded as a cold medium of exchange. A plain piece of silk deserves admiration for its shimmering softness alone, even if one is unaware of the skill required to reel and weave the gossamer filaments. And when diligent fingers have woven the colors into a lustrous design of birds or flowers or fabled beings, it becomes almost a living thing, sacred even when fresh from the loom. If, then, it has also served for a century or more before a temple altar or has covered an ancestral tea jar or was the ceremonial obi of a revered grandmother, it is indeed worthy of homage."

— Helen Benton Minnich in *Japanese Costume* Charles E. Tuttle Co., publisher; by permission.

a concentrated isolationism. This allowed her artistic traditions to continue undisturbed.

The relationship of dress to one's position in society, and the appreciation of the beauty of each individual textile, have always been important in Japan. Weavers worked to create masterpiece after masterpiece of silk *nishiki* — multicolored patterned silks using a variety of weaves. But technique is only a foil to design. The aim is not simply to create visual beauty, but also to evoke an emotion which, too, is experienced as beautiful.

Most interesting for the textile artist of today was the development of silk fabric dyeing in Japan, especially the paint – and – resist dyeing called *yuzen.* Other fabric dyeing techniques taken to their greatest elaboration: the tie-dye techniques of stitched and resisted areas known as *shibori,* and the use of *kanoka* – tiny tied dots – covering whole kimonos.

Today

At present, world production of silk is nearly as great as at any previous time, and it is increasing. Japan produces about 20,000 tons of raw-reeled silk a year and uses more than she can produce. Japan, Russia, India and China are all encouraging silk production in their spheres of influence to increase their supply of the raw material.

India produces large amounts of both cultivated and wild silks, most of which is used within the area. In much of the country sericulture and silk weaving are practiced on a small village scale, as they have been for millenia. India is probably the only place in the world where a large portion of pattern weaving is still done on hand and foot operated looms. The government even has a special agency that designs and strings up portable drawloom harnesses that village weavers then attach to their looms when they wish to weave a new pattern.

China has historically produced more silk than any other area of the world. And now, as only a small proportion is used domestically, China is undoubtedly the largest exporter of silk fiber and silk goods. Very little of this silk comes to the United States; most goes to Europe, where China's historic silk trade ties have been. Besides, until very recently the U.S. had a trade embargo on China.

Synthetics replaced silk in the U.S. popular market during World War II, when the sources of raw silk were cut off. The government subsidized the nylon industry because a silk substitute was imperative for parachutes and balloons. In the short time since then, silk has become an almost mythical fiber. It is being rediscovered by hand weavers, dyers and fiber artists as a unique medium. *Hurray for its return!*

Chapter 2

THE FIBER

Silks have always been the most desired of stuffs. They have been carried thousands of miles, where such journeys were dangerous, even deadly, and deemed worth it. For every bit of silk is a treasure. In the realm of fiber silk is as jewels.

hat are the qualities of silk that make it so esteemed? Paramount is its beauty: the natural beauty of the fiber, and the extraordinary colors it takes. Not only is it beautiful, it's also useful: silk makes the most comfortable clothes, and silk, while seemingly delicate, is actually one of the strongest, toughest fibers. And, too, silk is not the most abundant of stuffs. It takes proverbial effort and care to produce, process and weave it.

Silk is the most lustrous of the natural fibers. This luster is probably its most well known attribute. The luster comes from the way silk is formed. It is spun by the silk caterpillar as a semi-liquid, continuous filament that hardens on contact with air. The smooth surface of the silk fiber reflects light, and the reflected light is seen as luster.

The fiber is somewhat translucent, which gives depth to the reflection, so the luster seems warm, soft and deep.

Silk is also known for its lively sparkle. The surface of the fiber, while mostly smooth, does have small irregularities. These break up the reflected light and produce the sparkles.

One of the greatest joys of life is color. As a medium for color, silk is unsurpassed. The luster and depth of the fiber give luster and depth to colors, the sparkles give life. Silk colors are as beautiful as flowers. And silk is easy to dye.

The feel of silk is as delightful as its sight. It feels "silky", of course! But since our sense of what "silky" feels like may have been influenced by the now common synthetics, here is an experiment to try: go to a local fabric shop and feel fabric of different fibers. If there isn't any silk, then you'll have to bring some! Look for the rack of "silky" synthetics, and feel each of them. Scrunch them up, smooth them on your cheek, then feel the silk. The most pronounced difference is the warmth of the silk. Silk is soft and warm, yet refreshing; synthetics are glassy smooth and cold.

Silk is not only warm to touch, it is warm to wear. About as warm per weight as cashmere. Sweaters knit of bulky spun silk are a delight in winter, as warm and lightweight as down, with the advantage of the suppleness of knit. A shawl of silk, thinner and lighter than a shawl of wool, will keep one warmer. A shirt made of two layers of thin silk fabric is as warm as a bulkier wool, and it feels so nice. Insulation is, after all, what silk was created for.

On the other hand, in fashion circles silk is thought of as a summer fiber: lightweight fabrics, comfortable in warm, sultry weather because of their openness — the fiber itself seems to breathe. As one friend commented, "The trouble with silk is, when I wear it, I feel I have nothing on!"

Three physical factors cooperate for this cool-in-summer, warm-in-winter property: *hygroscopicity*, the ability to absorb moisture without feeling wet; a *low specific gravity* or density, that is, a low weight for volume; and the fiber's extraordinary *strength-in-fineness*.

Silk can absorb a phenomenal amount of moisture: 30% beyond its dry weight of water without feeling wet. This ability to take up moisture is common to all natural fibers in some degree. It is the biggest drawback of synthetics that they are not hygroscopic at all. As we always breathe moisture through the skin, it is important for clothes to be able to absorb it. Otherwise they feel clammy.

In Japan the method of keeping warm by using many layers of fine material took an interesting turn. At an early period, when the court was very rich, it became fashionable to wear one's wealth on one's back in the form of kimono on kimono. To be able to still move, each was very fine, thus, all the more troublesome and costly to weave. They were worn in such a way that the multiple layers, each in a different color, showed at collar, cuff and hem. Later, when such extravagence was no longer feasible, the appearance was maintained through thin strips sewn on at these places, the number of actual kimono worn being reduced from perhaps a dozen to two or three. Aesthetic was displayed, rather than gross wealth, for the arrangement of the colors showed one's artistic sense.

Wearing silk can have a profound effect on mood. Is this carrying things too far? Really, it's true! Put on a classic Chinese robe and one begins to feel so calm, dignified: the delicate silk! the exquisite embroidery! It is no wonder the repeated "Barbarian" invaders were so quickly absorbed into China: the new rulers put on those silk robes, and soon conformed their actions to the refined, calming clothes.

Silk is seductive in its mood. Almost everyone succumbs. From a weaver's Magical Jacket — "because I feel so magical wearing it" — to the exquisite kimono, to the flowing sari. Delicacy and calm.

There is no warmer, more comfortable clothing than thick woven or knit silks. If this is too much of an extravagance, a thin layer of silk under a thick layer of wool suffices. Old time loggers know that the way to keep feet toasty in the coldest, dampest Oregon weather is heavy wool socks, with thin silk ones inside. The Italians, who don't believe in eschewing comfort to climb mountains, manufacture thin silk-knit underwear just for pleasant mountaineering. There are even silk sleeping bags — top o' the line and very, very dear.

Silk is very light and airy because the molecular structure resembles a long string of ladders. Between the "steps" is air space. These tiny air spaces act both as insulation and as pores so that the silk can, in fact, "breathe".

Silk's extraordinary fineness can be used to weave gossamer summer fabrics, light as "woven wind". It can also be used to increase the fiber's natural ability to hold in warmth. A very thin but tight fabric can be woven from it, and multiple layers

> *"It will be sufficient here to note that a twisted thread of silk fibres, finer than the finest human hair, will stretch five or six inches to the yard, and bear a weight of from twelve to sixteen ounces. Also that a cable of silk would sustain a heavier weight than one of equal size composed of any other fibre."*
>
> —Luther Hooper

of the thin fabric, with the air space between, add to the insulation of the fiber itself, while keeping weight down.

Strength

Silk is very strong. As Hooper noted, a thread of silk, finer than a strand of hair, will hold up a pound weight, and, given equal diameters, a thread of silk is stronger than a thread of any other natural fiber. (Nylon is about as strong as silk; the other synthetic fibers are weaker.) Another common comparison is that a strand of silk is as strong as an iron wire of equal diameter; stronger than a steel wire of equal weight. This high tensile strength allows silk to be used in a very fine thread for weaving very thin, lightweight, but very strong fabric. A quintessential application of this property has been silk's use for parachutes.

A very clear understanding of silk's strength can be had by trying to break some reeled, or long-fibered spun, silk yarn. Compare the yarn's breaking resistance to that of same-diametered yarns of other fibers. (Compare diameters by rolling strands between thumb and forefinger.)

Silk's strength can even be annoying at times: if you catch a bit of fine reeled silk from a cut fabric edge, you can pull it out for quite a distance without even noticing you're caught on it. It's so light and delicate. Yet it's so strong it doesn't break.

As strong as it is, silk is a very fine fiber, and thus subject to wear through abrasion. It is tougher than cotton or fine wools like cashmere, whose fibers are about the same diameter as silk. But it is not as durable to abrasive wear as the bast fibers (linen, hemp, jute) or very coarse wools. Thus, silk carpets are for reclining, for touching, not for walking on . . . except maybe barefoot.

Elasticity

Silk is very elastic. It will stretch 10% to 20% over its length without breaking. And the fiber is like a spring, resilient to crushing as well as stretching. This gives fabric woven of silk the ability to stretch and mold itself, an attribute not usually found in woven cloth. This "give" is a great asset for clothing, especially tight fitting or tailored garments, sashes, cumberbunds, tight bodices and underclothes. It is also important that after such tension the fabric can spring back to its original shape. The elasticity of the silk fiber allows this: it springs back after being pulled or crushed out of shape.

That the fiber is stretchy makes it possible to knit with silk in the same way as with wool. That it is elastic helps the knit hold its original shape. Elasticity is very important to a well-functioning knit; while it's possible to knit with an inelastic fiber like linen, the results are equally inelastic.

High elasticity also means silk is the best fiber for weaving-warps that need a lot of stretch, strength and resiliency, as in drawloom, double-harness shedding, or for gauze, with its torturous twisting of the warp threads.

The silk molecule is "double sprung". There is a main, lengthwise coil and axilary side coils.

The long coil is a stretchable spring.

The axilary coils are compressible.
In a twisted thread they work together to make a very elastic and resilient yarn.

axilary springs   long springs
compressed   stretched

Durability

We've noted that silk, while seemingly delicate, is actually very tough and strong. Silk has another advantage in durability in that it is highly resistant to the various molds, mildews and rots that attack other fibers. For instance, I routinely soak silk for long periods to dye it, and in the winter a big skein of heavy silk yarn can take a week or more to dry. But there is never a problem of tendering, or of the stains and mildews one might expect with other fibers. That phenomenon commonly called "silk rot" is not a rot at all. It is the drastic tendering effect of the heavy over-weighting of silk with metal salts (see page 128), something that's fortunately no longer done. Common salt from perspiration can have this effect on any fiber if an article is worn and not washed for long periods.

The silk gum on raw silk is reportedly subject to molds and bacteria. Raw silk should be stored in a cool, dry place. However, I have had no problem with raw silk stored through Oregon winters, with no special precautions.

Silk is damaged by long periods in direct sunlight, as are all fibers. The wool moth does not attack silk. Silverfish will eat silk, but only if they're desperate; they much prefer cellulose fibers. Some carpet beetles eat silk, as well as wool and cellulose, so it is wise to examine stored silks occasionally. Mice *love* silk, and agree with people that it's the nicest stuff there is to line their nests.

Some of the oldest fragments of cloth that have been unearthed are the silks found in northern China. There, the cold and the natural durability of the silk have worked together to preserve the fragments. Most of the old textiles now preserved in museums and repositories are silk. Some of the reason for this is the durability of the fiber and some is its traditional use: the weaving of finest and fanciest fabrics, those which are naturally treasured.

---

sleeping in its bed
of silk
the caterpillar dreams
the butterfly

". . . vegetable fiber becomes worthless if mildew from dampness gets in its work, whereas silk is in its element when wet, as the following incident proves: In 1874 a silk mill was totally destroyed by the breaking of the reservoir dam, and sewing silk was scattered for miles below, and has been plowed up by farmers frequently since and found to have its original strength. A tangled mass, weighing several pounds, was found in 1901, having been 27 years in the mud at the bottom of the mill pond. After washing and drying the color (black) was good, its luster fair, and its strength unimpaired."

—The Corticelli Silk Company

Schapping
"The method is as follows: If waste silk is piled in a heap in a damp, warm place, and kept moist and warm, the gum will in a few days' time begin to ferment and loosen, and can then be washed off, leaving the true thread soft and supple; but the smell caused by the fermentation is so offensive that it cannot be practised in or near towns. Therefore schappe spinners place their degumming plant in the hills, near a stream of pure water."

—Encyclopedia Britannica, Eleventh edition

Soap Degumming
is a process similar to the scouring of wool: the raw silk is simmered in a soapy bath until the gum is dissolved, then the soapy solution is rinsed out.

What's in a name?
what an aura surrounds that term "Raw Silk".
Excitement . . . adventure . . . luxury
visions of nomads, head to the wind, tracking across vast
*   deserts*
camel caravans
then moutains: towering crags, range after range to be
*   crossed*
by walking up ledges no more than one man wide
"roads" built and wound by men for centuries
millenia?
tiny ledges of rubble clinging —
climbing the mountain's twisted side

treasures transported on men's backs
raw, indeed

Raw Silk

Silk as it comes from the cocoon is coated with a protective layer called silk gum, or sericin. The coating may be any color: white, yellow, brown, beige, green; its color is not related to the color of the silk beneath it. The silk gum is dull and stiff, so it is usual to remove it to reveal the pure, lustrous, soft silk fiber. Silk with all its gum is called *raw silk.* Raw silk is silk in its strongest, most elastic and most durable state.

There are several processes for removing the silk gum. Called "degumming", "stripping", "boiling off" or "schapping", the process may remove all the gum, or only a portion. Silk which retains some gum is stronger in all respects than if the gum is completely removed. Partial degumming will give a silk whose luster is softly muted. *Schapping* is a special process of fermentation which gives a silk as soft and lustrous as fully degummed silk, while retaining a portion of the gum. *Soupling* is another process which gives a soft silk while retaining almost all the gum.

True raw silk should not be confused with the fashionable "raw silk" fabric, actually woven from noil silk (see pages 54 and 103).

The Source of Silk

Silk has always been costly. A great amount of labor is needed to raise the silkworms. It takes about a month from hatching of egg to cocoon, during which time the caterpillars must be fed ever increasing amounts of hand-picked mulberry leaves. Should the leaves be dirty, they must be washed, then carefully dried. Uncontrollable factors such as damp weather or sudden cold can make the worms sick; any setback to their growth and health will lower the quality and amount of silk produced.

About two full-grown mulberry trees and 4,000 eggs are needed to produce 12 pounds of cocoons (*Fessenden*). The proportion of raw reeled silk to cocoons varies greatly as the reelability of the cocoons depends on the strength of the fiber and its uniformity, the proportion of silk to chrysalis, and whether the cocoons are weighed fresh or dry. A usual ratio is 12:1 — 12 pounds of cocoons give one pound reeled silk, plus about an equal amount of unreelable spinning silk. In Japan, where great care is given to silk production, the ratio is about 6:1. Italy, at the turn of the century and the height of its silk industry, was said to produce cocoons with a reelability of 3:1 or 4:1.

Modern breeding and management of both the mulberry and silk caterpillars in Japan has doubled the production of silk per acre of mulberries during the last 20 years. The average yearly crop is about 600 pounds of cocoons per acre, yielding about 100 pounds of raw reeled silk plus some spinning fiber. These figures are based on two rearing periods a year, one as early in the spring as possible and one as late in the fall. The mulberries are trained as bushes for easy picking. Precise yield figures aren't available for other countries and situations, but an oft given estimate is 150 pounds fresh cocoons per acre per rearing, yielding 12 pounds raw reeled silk and 12 pounds spinning fiber (*Fessenden* and *Williams*).

> "The natural supply of silk for the whole world for, say, 4,000 years, the monetary value of which is incalculable, has depended almost entirely upon the instinct of the caterpillar of a most inconspicuous moth to provide for itself a snug case in which its metamorphosis into its perfect form might be effected."
> —Luther Hooper

Silkworm rearing obtains the raw material, the cocoons. Then the silk must be carefully reeled, and at some point de-gummed and re-reeled. The re-reeling is probably the most difficult work: the fiber is fine, easily tangled and broken. When done by hand it is usual for a skilled re-reeler to complete one-half pound in a full day's work. Fortunately, most of this work can be mechanized.

Consider the work involved, and it is amazing that silk does not cost more. Cost is kept down because most of the silk

---

"The gold and silver spider are both found in Rhodesia, South Africa.

"The gold spider spins its web (not in cocoon) of golden thread, and lets it float from the trees. Sometimes these webs are twenty feet long; they strike other branches. Then they stretch from branch to branch, or from tree to tree, making a gorgeous appearance in the tropical sun. The fiber of this web is of great fineness.

"The silver spider spins a less beautiful web. It is spun from bush to bush, or from one tree to another, but it is not left to float loosely. It is not so strong as the golden spider's thread, though very beautiful.

"These spiders live on flies, which are very abundant in that country."

—Mrs. Carrie Williams

Spider Silk

The nests and webs of spiders are also silk. Spider silk is raised for use as hair lines in telescopes and optical instruments, as the strand spun by certain spiders is the finest natural filament known. (Surpassed only recently by threads drawn from molten rock crystal.)

Raising spiders for silk in quantity is not considered practical. As they are carnivores, their food would be far more costly than the vegetation eaten by silk caterpillars. It would be interesting, though, to gather some of this type wild silk and spin it. The common, large black and yellow garden spider (Miranda aurentia) is considered one of the best types.

Rima's dresses in William Henry Hudson's *Green Mansions* were of spider silk.

---

raising of the world is done where wages are very low. Traditionally, in the Orient, silk was the cash crop of the small farmer. At the turn of the century it was estimated that every other farm in both China and Japan raised a crop of worms each summer. Perhaps one pound of raw silk would be realized from the month's work, which was usually done by the women and children of the family. In southern China, mulberry trees grow like weeds in waste places, so no extra land was used for them. In other places, as in Japan, mulberries were planted along country lanes and ditches, just as pollarded charcoal trees lined lanes in Italy.

Wild Silk

There are really two distinct types of silk, the cultivated kind just discussed and the wild kinds. They differ in several qualities. The most striking is that wild silk is usually not white, it is colored. The shade may vary from an off-white through light yellow to a fairly dark gray, but it is most often a light to medium beige. The color comes from the diet of the wild caterpillars. Instead of delicate mulberry leaves they may eat oak, plum, jujube or castor bean plant. These leaves are full of tannin and the tannin becomes a part of the silk, coloring it.

Wild silk is usually called *tussah* silk. Actually tussah (tussore, tassar, tassah) silk is a very abundant type of wild silk. While most commercially available wild silk is tussah silk, there are also uncountable other kinds of wild silks, each with its own peculiarities and characteristics: one may be very dark but dye well; another may be perfectly white yet not take to dyeing; some are fine, some are strong, some are reelable, some are not, and some have distinctive smells to them.

Each species or variety of wild silk caterpillar feeds on certain plants and forms cocoons and fiber of distinctive color and type. One variety, the Assam or munga worm, is known for producing a range of colors and quality according to what is eaten. The lightest and most delicate, off the champaca tree, is said to rival cultivated silk. Another cultivated type of wild silk is the Yama-mai of Japan. The cocoons are green, the silk is white, and it is the strongest and most elastic of all silks. In times past, royal families might reserve to their own use the finest varieties of local wild silks.

Wild silk can be found anywhere, as any caterpillar which spins a cocoon is spinning silk. The most renowned and commercially gathered kinds flourish in the tropical, sub-tropical and warm-temperature regions of Asia. There are species of caterpillars in the United States that yield a useable quantity and quality of wild silk. Keep an eye out for cocoon clusters, large caterpillars or moths, and you may find some near you.

Wild silk is a coarser fiber than cultivated silk. This makes it more durable to wear, thus more practical for clothing and other wear-subject uses. Traditionally it has been used for pile fabrics and carpets. Every silk Oriental carpet I have seen, also the marvelous chenille imitations from Scotland, have been of wild silk. Usually its shade is a very light grayed beige, so light that it would probably be thought of as an aged white or else a dyed off-white. Dyed, it mutes the colors only just enough to make them slightly more subtle. It is rarely recognized for what it is: wild silk.

Because it grows free, without cultivation, and needs only to be gathered and processed, wild silk is usually less expensive than cultivated white silk. It is also rarely reeled, since, in order to assure a continuing supply, the cocoons are gathered after the moth has emerged. The cocoons are pulled apart and the fiber is carded and spun like wool or cotton. Spinning rather than reeling makes for less cost, and means that yarns can be made in sizes like wool or cotton, heavy enough to be very attractive to the hand craftsman.

Think of wild silk as a more substantial fiber than cultivated silk, yet with all the other great silk qualities. It can be handled like a fine-staple wool and used in weaving, knitting, crochet, stitchery — all techniques, really, in the same ways as wool or cotton. This familiar *handl*ing is a great attraction of wild silk.

A good percentage, about half, of white silk fiber also is spun: the fiber at the outside and inside of each cocoon that cannot be reeled; all breeding cocoons from which the moths are allowed to emerge; and all waste from breakage. These go to make yarns which, like spun wild silk, are of a size easily handled, and they are in the same cost range as the wild silk yarns.

Silkworms of the World

Bombyx Mori – "cocoon producing, mulberry-eating". THE domesticated silkworm. There are many races, divided into: *uni-voltine* – one generation is raised in a year; *poly-voltine* – two or more generations may be raised in a year. The univoltine are also divided into strains for spring or autumn rearing.

There are many other cultivated *Bombyx*, all mulberry feeding, and more or less domesticated in India. Most are polyvoltine, and all produce reelable cocoons. For example: The **Chinese Monthly** – *Bombyx sinensis* – polyvoltine; small cocoon, but prolific. Many other mulberry feeding Bombyx are not cultivated, but may be gathered as wild silk.

Tussahs

The **Saturnids** or **Giant Silkworm Moths** are the best known of the wild silk moths. They are large moths with distinctive "eye" markings on their wings.

Chinese Tussah or tussur moth – *Antheraea pernyi* – is a native of China and Manchuria. It eats oak leaves, mainly of the *Quercus serrata*, with color and quality of the silk dependent on climate and soil: the cold weather of Manchuria gives a dark, heavy cocoon; the mild climate and sandy soil of Shantung give a lighter colored and lighter weight cocoon.

Indian Tussah – *Antheraea mylitta* – is closely related to the Chinese tussah. It lives throughout the whole of India and feeds mainly on the jujube tree. The cocoon is very large – 2" long by 1" diameter – and can be reeled, although it rarely is. The silk is said to have a strong, characteristic odor.

Bombyx Mori

Chinese Tussah

Other Wild Silks

Yama-mai silk – *Antheraea (Samia) yama-mai* – The Yama-mai worm of Japan. Oak feeding. The cocoon is large and bright green. The silk is white, very strong and elastic. But it is not so easily bleached or dyed as *Bombyx mori* silk. Formerly reserved for the exclusive use of the Imperial family.

Munga silk – *Antheraea assama* – The munga or mooga worm of Assam. Somewhat domesticated. The fiber is generally a dark brownish color, but this varies widely according to the worms' food. The silk from the champaca tree (*Michelia champaca*) is a fine white fiber known as **Champa Pattea Moonga**. It was formerly reserved for the exclusive use of the Rajahs. The dark mooga silk is difficult to bleach, but it takes dye very well – more deeply and more evenly than either tussah or eria silk. The moth is large, the female much larger than the male, and they are handsomely marked. The cocoon is also large, almost 2" long.

Eri or **Eria** silk — *Attacus ricini* — Eria or arrindi moth of Bengal, Assam and Nepal. Feeds on the castor oil plant, and probably could be cultivated wherever castor beans will grow. Polyvoltine, with up to seven generations a year. The cocoons are loose and flossy, orange-red or sometimes white. **Assam Eria** is well known for being very white and of good quality. **Singapore Eria** is brown. It is difficult to dye. Eria silk is spun, as the loose cocoons cannot be reeled.

Cynthia moth — *Attacus cynthia* — Domesticated in China, where it eats *Ailanthus glandulosa* (Chinese sumach).

Ailanthus silkworm of Europe is a cross of *A. cynthia* and *A. ricini,* first bred by Guérin Méneville and now spread throughout the silk growing regions of Europe.

Atlas moth — *Attacus atlas* — An omnivorous caterpillar (very unusual, as most caterpillars are vegetarians) found throughout India, especially in the south, Ceylon, Burma, China and Java. One of the largest of the silk moths, up to 10" across at the wings. Its cocoons are open at one end.

Selene silk — *Actias selene* — Indian **Moon Moth**. Spins a huge cocoon, 3" long.

Anaphe silk — *Anaphe*, species — found in Uganda and other parts of Africa. Feeds on fig leaves. Constructs large nests with clusters of cocoons inside them. The whole nest is used for spinning. In Nigeria, anaphe silk is used with cotton for making **Soyan** cloth.

Luna

Polyphemus

Cecropia

North American Wild Silks

Asian **Ailanthus** silk moth—*Philosamia (Attacus) walkeri (cynthia)*. Was introduced to the East Coast around 1861. It eats ailanthus (Chinese sumach), wild cherry, sycamore, lilac and other tree leaves. The caterpillar is green, with black, blue and yellow markings. Cocoons are spun in a leaf, secured to the branch with silk. The pupa overwinters in the cocoon.

Polyphemus moth—*Telea (Antheraea) polyphemus*—caterpillars eat oak, birch and other leaves. They are greenish, with diagonal stripes on the sides of the largest segments. The moths' wings are ochre, sometimes pinkish, each with a transparent spot. The hind wing spots are partially bordered with blue and are set in a black ring. The cocoon is reelable, and considered the most potentially valuable of our native wild silks.

Cecropia moth—*Samia (Hyalophora) cecropia*—the caterpillar is about 4" long, green, with blue, yellow and red markings. It eats many different plants, resulting in silks of varying qualities. Cocoons are large, double layered, and are fastened lengthwise to branches. The Cecropia moth is very large and distinctive. Its body is banded red and white. Wings are mainly reddish brown, with markings in red, black and white. The span is about 5"-6". Cecropias are common in the Atlantic and Plains states, and there are related species in the west and Canada.

Promethea or **Spice Bush** moth—*Callosamia promethea*—caterpillar eats spice-bush and related deciduous plants. It is 2"-3" long with yellow-green head, blue-green body, and markings in black, yellow and red. Cocoons are like the Ailanthus' but are darker and slimmer. Moths are smaller than Cecropia, the male an almost black dark maroon, the female marked similar to Cecropia. A related species feeds on the tulip tree.

Luna or **Moon** moth—*Actias (Tropoea) luna*—A large and striking light green moth with long "tails". The caterpillar eats walnut, hickory, liquid-amber and other leaves. It is about 3" long and green colored. The rather thin cocoon is made between leaves on the ground.

Io moth—*Automeris (Hyperchiria) io*—the caterpillars are green with a red and white stripe down each side. Their tufts of sharp spines will sting. They eat many plants including corn. The cocoon is thin, semi-transparent and brown. It is spun on the ground.

Rothschildia—A group of South and Central American silk moths with some species found as far north as Arizona.

Raising Silk

The raising of a few score silkworms can be a real treat. It's a fairly common science project for primary grades, and some people raise cocoons to reel off the silk for their traditional Japanese embroidery. Silkworms are raised for scientific investigations, where they are used like insect guinea pigs. Two main strains have been developed, one very hardy, one very delicate. Neither of them was bred for silk quality, but the hardy strain would be very good for first attempts at silk raising. The Japanese have scores of silkworm strains, developed for special qualities of the fiber (tenacity, elasticity, diameter, yield) or environmental situations.

The preferred food of the silkworm is the white mulberry, *Morus alba*, but they will happily eat other mulberries' leaves if the *Morus alba* isn't available. For instance, the East Indian mulberry, *Morus multicaulis*, is common in the southern United States and is an acceptable food. While it is said Osage Orange and even lettuce leaves will sustain the worms, they will not produce much useable silk on such a diet.

An interesting point is that silk raising can be carried out in the city. All that's needed is a supply of mulberry trees sufficient to feed the number of worms you are raising, and the dedication to feed them night and day for the final week of their lives.

Raising Tussah

In China, TUSSAH silk is semi-cultivated. The oaks whose leaves the caterpillars eat are pruned to grow as shrubs, five to six feet high, with the worms raised directly on the trees.

Mature caterpillars are three to five inches long, and are a soft green with tufts of reddish brown hair.

Two annual crops are raised: the small spring crop is used to breed the large autumn crop. Then most of the autumn crop is reeled.

The worm over-winters in the cocoon, emerging as a moth to mate in the early spring.

Expected yield is about 40 pounds of raw-reeled silk per acre of oak trees, plus about 60 pounds of spinning fiber.

Identification

Burn Test. The simplest identification test for silk fiber, and a portable one, is the burn test. Take a bit of the yarn, or twist up a bit of spinning fiber, or take off a length of the constituent yarns of the fabric under question. Hold the bit, preferably in some tweezers, and light the end with a match flame. Smell the smoke of the burning fiber. The animal fibers, silk and wool, will smell like ammonia. They are made of protein, and the nitrogen component of protein is given off as ammonia on burning. Cellulose fibers, cotton, linen and rayon, will smell like burnt paper. Nylon has a very strong characteristic smell, but the smell of polyester and acrylics is not so pronounced. Observe proper safety when doing these burn tests.

Different fibers also burn in different manners. Wool and silk are naturally flame resistent. They burn slowly for the size of the sample (thin samples will burn more quickly), and they will stop burning — self-extinguish — when the flame is removed. A black ball of charred, melted material is left at the end of the sample. Cellulose fibers and synthetics burn readily and sometimes flare up, so be cautious. Nylon will melt more quickly than it will burn.

By Sight. Silk can be distinguished visually from other fibers by its combination of luster and pin point sparkles. Wool, linen and mercerized cotton may have a nice luster, but they do not sparkle. Synthetics, such as viscose rayon, may have a lot of sparkle, but when they are examined closely in natural light, the sparkles are seen as lines, the reflection of a length of fiber. With silk the sparkles are pin points, scattered along the fiber. This distinction won't hold if the silk still has a coat of gum, as the silk gum masks the sparkles.

The dimensions of the fibers are only a limited guide. The diameters of fine wool and cotton are close to the range of silk. Rayon is usually spun more coarsely. The length of the fiber can be of help. Cotton is always short, 1½" or less, and fine wools would rarely be over 4". Should the staple be longer, then it would have to be either silk or synthetic.

By Feel. A very good way to tell silk from other fibers is by *how it feels.* Silk's feel is quite distinctive, but it has to be learned by experience, so feel away. I can analyze my sensations, but they may differ from yours; and the distinctions are subtle, so they can be taken only as a guide.

1. Surface. Silk has a smoothness, even if rough spun, that distinguishes it from cotton and wool. Yet the smoothness is not glassy, as is the rayon and nylon synthetics'. They feel harsh compared to silk. Polyesters and acrylics feel cloying to me, almost greasy. Cotton feels dry.

2. Hand-resiliency. Silk is more resilient than any other fiber. The resiliency of silk shows if you tightly crumple up a handful of silk fabric, then quickly open your hand. Silk will spring out; fabric of other fibers will open up only slowly. This unique spring of tightly wadded silk fabric was as important to its use in parachutes as was its strength.

3. Temperature. Given all the fibers at the same room temperature, silk feels warmer to the hand than most other fibers. Occasionally a napped cotton feels as warm as silk, but usually cotton, linen, and especially the sleek synthetics, are pronouncedly cooler. Wool feels warmer, and this is true of even the sleek wools like mohair and alpaca. Acrylics (imitation wool) feel warmer than silk, but their greasy feel gives them away.

4. Catchiness. If your hands are rough, fine silks will catch on the rough places. This is especially true of lightweight and fine silks, both yarns and fabrics, but is not so characteristic of tightly twisted yarns or tightly woven fabrics like pongee and taffeta. Rayons are not nearly so catchy, while fine nylon, such as is used for clothing knits and stockings, seems even catchier than silk, although in a slightly different way.

Lye Test

A hot lye solution will dissolve all animal fibers in 10 to 15 minutes.

Dissolve one tablespoon of lye in a half cup cold water in a stainless steel or unchipped enamel pan. Add a small piece of the yarn/fiber/fabric. Warm slowly. Avoid splattering any lye about.

White silk will dissolve very quickly, some wild silks may take longer. Wool will also dissolve quickly, but the cellulose/synthetic fibers will remain, more or less unchanged, although some swell and most turn yellow.

Rayon and some other synthetics weaken when wet — silk does not.

wet here and pull

Such synthetics will break at the wet place.

Silk from Wool

It is usually possible to distinguish silk from wool by sight and feel. Cashmere and some alpaca would be the only wools fine enough, "silky" enough and without the characteristic crimp of the finer sheeps wools, that they might want distinguishing. Both of these are the under-fleece of a hairy top coat. In the processing some hairs always slip by and end up in the yarn. So look for the presence of these occasional hairs.

A chemical test to distinguish wool from silk is to put it in cold concentrated sulphuric acid (H_2SO_4). This should dissolve everything easily, except for wool. Wool is attacked slowly, while the scales on the surface of the wool fiber become more visible.

Another test is to immerse in a solution of oxide of lead. The wool darkens, due to the sulphur it contains.

Cultivated silk is said to be distinguished from wild silk by the action of cold, concentrated hydrochloric acid (HCl). The white silk is dissolved, while the wild is only slightly affected.

A small low power microscope is a great aid to identifying fibers, as each can be distinguished by its surface character.

Cultivated silk is a smooth, continuous double strand. It appears smooth, almost glassy, and translucent. It also shows a slight prismatic, rainbow effect.

Wild silk is very similar, but the double strands are themselves made up of numerous long smooth fibrils that give it an appearance of lengthwise striation. And tussah fibers are thicker than white silk fibers.

Bast fibers appear striated crosswise. Cotton has a characteristic ribbon-like twist. The wool fiber's surface is made up of overlapping scales.

Synthetics are very regular — far more regular than even the smoothest reeled silk.

Chapter 3

REELED & SPUN

here are two basic types of silk yarns, the **thrown** and the **spun.** They correspond to the two basic forms of the fiber, **reeled** and **cut.** "Throwing" is the process of twisting the unspun filaments of reeled silk, so such silk is called thrown silk.

Thrown silk is almost always cultivated silk. Some Chinese tussah is reeled for pongee, but virtually all other wild silk cocoons are gathered after the moth has emerged and are not reelable. Also, only about half of each cultivated cocoon is reelable; the rest becomes staple to be spun. These two factors, the necessity of cultivation and the large amount of unreelable waste, together with the great care which must be taken in the reeling, throwing and degumming operations, mean that thrown silk will necessarily be very expensive. That it is so very beautiful makes it worth the expense.

Thrown Silk Yarns

Thrown silk yarns are rarely available to handweavers. This is partly due to their expense, since expensive yarns are rarely popular and yarns which are not popular are rarely stocked by suppliers, and it is partly due to the fact that thrown silk yarns are usually very fine, much finer than most of us are comfortable with.

Sometimes reeled silk is available as raw silk. Raw silk has an interesting texture. It can be used as is, and it will eventually wear soft and glossy. Though raw silk is stiff, and therefore may be difficult to handle, fabric can be woven in the raw, then piece degummed.

Many available silk fabrics are woven of thrown silk. These fabrics will be stronger and more durable than comparable fabrics of spun silk. The long filaments allow a yarn of very little twist, so the fabric may be highly lustrous and soft. And the long, strong filaments can be woven into fabric so thin it is transparent.

The most important generic terms for thrown silk yarns are *organzine* and *tram.* Organzine is tightly twisted and plied, and is used for warp. Tram is given only enough twist to keep it together; it is used for weft.

Another major kind of reeled silk is *duppioni* — silk reeled from double cocoons. It is regular, in the main, but every so often large slubs from where the two cocoons were joined are brought up into the yarn. Fabric woven from it is considered very subdued and elegant in a robust sort of way.

Manufacture of Reeled Silk

For millenia silk has been reeled by hand. In this very simple way, one hand guides the thread, the other turns the reel. The cocoons float in a basin of water to soften the gum and allow the filament to pull off. Even this simple method was a great improvement over the first unreelings, where a cocoon was held in the mouth to soften, and the filament wound on the fingers or a stick. *(Minnich)*

Industrial refinements began in the 14th century in Europe. The improvements were a mechanically turned reel, a steam heated water basin, and a method of twisting the thread about itself. These improved both the speed and regularity of the reeling process and the resulting thread. Silk became the first industrial fiber. The improvements lowered its cost relative to other fibers which were all still spun completely by hand. This mechanization, mild though it was, greatly contributed to the wider availability of silk in Europe and its eventual status as a popular fiber. It could be more than just a luxury for the very rich.

To prepare them for reeling, cocoons are cleaned of the outer floss: the silk hammock that attached the cocoon to the branch on which it was spun. Then they are soaked in near boiling water to soften the gum, and the cocoon is gone over lightly with a little brush until an end is caught. Several ends are taken to form the thread, according to its desired size.

The Chinese symbol for "fine, delicate" is a thread being reeled from two cocoons, the very finest thread possible. Usually a minimum of four ends are reeled together. For a given size yarn, the number of cocoons needed will vary according to their quality, the size of the filament, and whether one is reeling the main portion or the end of the cocoon. The middle portion is the largest diameter, the end (inside of cocoon) is thinnest. A new end is attached to the reeled thread whenever it is judged to be getting a little thin.

Filatures

In hand reeling, the filaments are simply gathered and reeled. The French Chambon, and the Italian Tavelette systems of reeling improve this by twisting the yarn on itself, to form a rounder, more compact and uniform thread. In both these systems the distance between basin and skein is increased, so despite the greater speed of a mechanically turned reel, the thread can dry before it reaches the skein. This makes re-reeling easier.

The grouping of several basins together into a *filature* — silk reeling house — where heat could be uniformly maintained by steam, was an important step. When the cocoon soaking water varies in temperature the reeling proceeds irregularly and the thread is not uniform: filaments have a greater tendency to break and pull up loops and the color, strength, diameter and elasticity of the raw silk filament will vary slightly with the changing temperature. For this reason, hand reeled silk, even though more care and skill go into it, will be much less regular than filature or "steam" silk.

For several hundred years the form of the filature was fairly standard. One girl attended one basin — one reeling thread. She had to be skilled in judging the size of the thread in order to know when to add another cocoon end, and vigilant to catch any irregularities or breaks in the filaments. A less skilled girl, working up to be a reeler, "groped" the ends, and provided prepared cocoons to the reelers. Beginning workers pulled off the floss-hammock. A supervisor attended several girls/basins. Someone else gathered up the waste silk.

The greatest advantage to this filature reeling, over hand reeling, is that it went faster. Each basin still required one person to attend it. But the machine-turned reel could turn at an average of 100 revolutions per minute, skeining about 100 yards. At such a speed one cocoon takes about five minutes to reel off. For comparison, Jean Case suggests allowing two hours to reel the same amount by hand, using a niddy-noddy. Even with all these improvements, only 10 to 12 ounces per day would be reeled from each basin.

Such were the filatures, with some small additions, from the 17th century to about the 1920's when multi basins per person began to be used. Today, with automatic "gropers" and

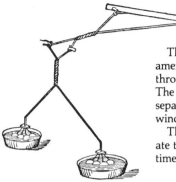

The Chambon

The silk is reeled in pairs of skeins. The filaments rise from a pair of basins and pass through glass eyes that gather the threads. The two threads twist about each other, are separated, twist about each other again, then wind onto two skeins.

This system is considered more appropriate to finer threads, averaging four ends at a time, to give yarns up to 12 deniers.

The Tavelle or Tavellette

One basin is used, reeling one skein at a time. The thread rises from the basin through a glass eye, up to a spool, down to a second spool, then it is twisted on itself, around the part going from the eye to the first (top) spool. It then goes up to a hook and over to the skein.

This system is better for 13 deniers yarns and above, using eight ends (cocoons) or so.

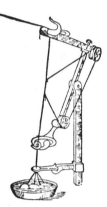

Silk Reel.

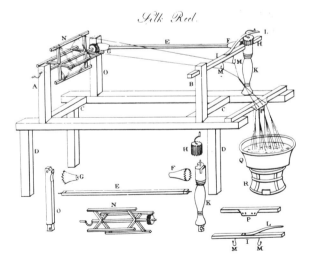

end placers, automatic feeders of cocoons to basins, automatic temperature regulators, and a device to keep track of the diameter of the thread, the fully automatic filature is complete. One person can attend to a huge machine of a hundred basins.

Manufacture of Spun Silk

The manufacture of spun silk is relatively modern. Formerly, waste silk was used for wadding, where it provides insulation just like down. It was handspun to some extent by the silk raisers themselves, in order to make use of the pierced breeder cocoons. Prior to the development of wool and cotton spinning machinery, reeled silk was the only fiber whose preparation was mechanized at all. This same wool and cotton machinery provided the apparatus for the widespread spinning of short staple silk.

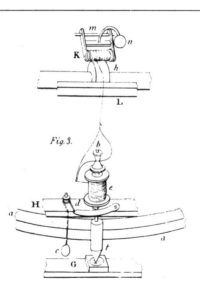

A Single Spindle From A Twisting Machine
a-a turns t which turns bobbin e-b. The twirling of bobbin e-b gives twist to the roving as it moves off of e, through the wire eyes of b and up onto K. K is turned by means of h. n and d-c are weighting devices which keep the two bobbins pressed up to their turners. The faster e-b turns, relative to K, the more twist is imparted to the yarn.

The manufacture of silk fiber for spinning requires that the pierced cocoons or loose fiber first be degummed. Raw silk is too stiff to spin well. And the silk gum not only coats the fibers, it also glues them together, making it impossible to card the fibers without first degumming them. The fermentation process called schapping is often used in Europe. In England and the United States, soap or soda degumming is used. The process is similar to scouring wool: the fiber is boiled in an alkaline solution that strips off the silk gum. Care in degumming the inside as well as the outside of the cocoons is important although any unevenness can be corrected after spinning by a final degumming known as "boiling off". After being well rinsed, the cocoons are dried in a hydro-extractor, which works like the "spin" cycle in a washing machine.

Next the cocoons or loose fibers are "dressed". They are pulled apart by running them between rollers and a wire-studded cylinder, like a very large drum carder. The spinning caterpillar lays out the silk fiber in rows of "figure-eights": ୪୫୫୫୫୫୫. The next operation runs the silk through more rollers that pull out the figure-eights and lay the fibers smoooth and parallel. They are then cut into uniform lengths and draped over rods; these "flags" are combed to remove dirt and short fibers. Then they are combined into the long laps that handspinners know as rovings or tops.

Mill spinning separates the process of drawing out and twisting that are done simultaneously in handspinning. First, the fat laps are drawn out into thinner and thinner "slivers": the lap is fed through two sets of rollers, the second set revolving faster than the first. For evenness, several slivers are combined and run through the process again, perhaps several times. The sliver, which also may be called a roving, is wound onto bobbins from which it is twisted.

The sliver is twisted into a singles as it is drawn off the top of the revolving bobbin. To ply the singles, they are first wound two together, then they are twisted again, but in the opposite direction.

The finished thread is sometimes "gassed": run very quickly through a small gas flame, which singes off the fuzzy fiber ends. This increases the smoothness and luster of the yarn.

Spun Silk Names

Spun silk yarns go by many names: some refer to the fiber-length, some to the fiber's character, and some to the yarn's spin. The relationship of name to reality is not always consistent, so it is better to examine a yarn for its actual characteristics than to rely on names. Here are some of the more common terms:

Tussah (tussur, tussore, etc.) is used for all wild silks.

Schappe refers to the European fermentation process of degumming, and also may be used loosely for "spun silk".

Boiled-Off means fully degummed; partially degummed silks are very softly lustrous; luster and sparkle are increased by boiling-off.

Meche implies a fairly soft, regularly twisted, long staple white silk.

Shantung may be used for a slightly slubby, usually white, silk. It is also used for reeled duppioni silk.

Cord or *Cordonnet* is a tightly twisted and plied, dense and rounded cord-like silk.

Floss is softly twisted, so it will press down flat. It may be used for spun or reeled silk. Floss is also used for the first pre-reelable fibers of the cocoon, said to be extra strong and soft.

Flourette is long staple and spun of combed fibers.

Bourette is short staple (1"-2") and spun of carded fibers.

Noil is very short staple and contains little tangle-balls of fiber.

Spun Silk Yarns — Counts

Spun silk yarns are sized or numbered according to several systems. The most commonly used now is the metric. The number, or count, is written x/y, where x refers to the size of the singles of which the yarn is made, and y refers to how many of these singles are twisted together to make the yarn. The size of the singles is figured as the number of thousands of meters required to weigh a kilo (2.2 pounds).

For instance, a 10/2 m.c. ("metric count"), at 5000 meters per kilo (theoretical), will have about half the yardage (meterage?) of a 10/1, at 10,000 meters per kilo (theoretical). Working yardage is always less — usually about 5% less — because the count is measured with the yarn fully stretched.

Reeling Tussah Silk in China

The Chinese tussah silk worm *(A. pernyi)* over-winters in the cocoon. Reeling is done during this over-wintering dormancy as then the open end of the cocoon is sealed with silk gum.

Tussahs have more gum and calcium compounds than mulberry silks, so before reeling the cocoons are boiled in sodium carbonate for 1½ hours, rinsed and reboiled in fresh water, then soaked about 16 hours longer.

The reeling is done with the cocoons in a semi-dry condition: they lie on a board rather than float in a basin. The freshest cocoons are the easiest to reel.

All the reeling is done in very hot and humid rooms, by men. Foot power reels are used. Usually eight ends are reeled together by the Tavalette system to give 30/35 deniers yarn.

(Huber, in Mathews' 1943 edition)

There is also a difference due to plying. For instance, a 20/2 m.c., approximately 4200 yd/lb, has slightly less working yardage than a 10/1 m.c., approximately 4400 yd/lb. The plied yarn will have a little less actual yardage, because the singles making up a plied yarn lose some length to the plying twist.

The English have a different system: the number is also written x/y. The x refers to the number of 840 yard hanks needed to weigh one pound, and y tells the number of plies. A size 10 yarn will always have the same yardage no matter how many singles went to make it.

Not to leave things too orderly, sometimes the number of plies is given first.

Reclining Woman. Redrawn from an Indian miniature, mid-18th century, illustrating the evening raga *Varari* (sensual longing).

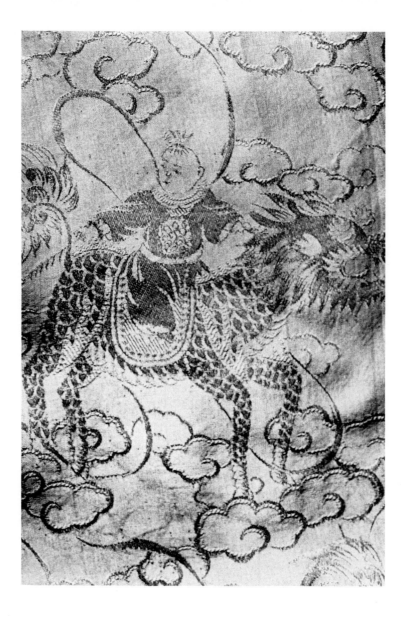

PLATE I. *Boy Riding Mythical Beast Through the Clouds.*
Southeast Asia, early 20th century. Damask of satin and
plain weave. Natural white. Detail, approximately full
size. PHOTO BY JOHN BAUGUESS.

PLATE II. *Vase carpet.* Charles Smith, USA, 1978. Knotted pile. Naturally dyed silk and wool: light blue-green silk ground; natural tussah border; flowers in many colors, especially reds, plums and darker blues. Size: 30″×42″. PHOTO BY CHARLES SMITH.

PLATE III. *Zapoteca.* From the mountains outside Oaxaca, spinning local wild silk. PHOTO BY JAMES BASSLER.

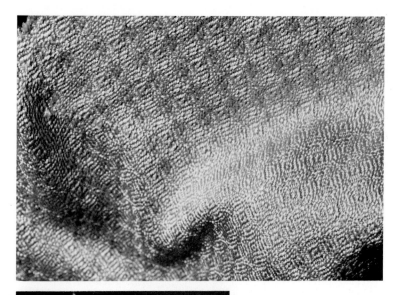

PLATE IV. *Mary's Flowers.* Elaine and Hal Cutcher, USA, 1975. Dobby woven wedding dress fabric. Glossy white soft-twist tram was used for both warp and weft, resulting in a cloth of indescribable softness. Scale: 1:2. PHOTO BY JOHN BAUGUESS.

Silk Woman. Jan Sousa, USA, 1978. Moulded silk and cotton paper, with silk fibers. PHOTO BY JAN SOUSA.

PLATE V. *Cherry Blossoms.* Japan, 20th century. Silk scarf
used for obi tie. Damask of satin and crêpe. Rose tan with
white resist-dyed flowers. Detail, approximately full size.
PHOTO BY JOHN BAUGUESS.

PLATE VI. *Dragon gauze.* China, 20th century. Sha-type gauze with roundel of two dragons. This type of gauze was used as inserts in the sleeves of Mandarin robes. Size of roundel: 7″ × 8″. PHOTO BY JOHN BAUGUESS.

Plate VII. *Bridal lace.* Maltese bobbin lace, brought from England in the early 1900s. A design formed by areas of slightly distorted plain weave, connected by lace loops. Because the "plain weave" is formed by a kind of plaiting, it is far less regular than loomed plain weave, and has more depth of texture. When the veil is worn, the design floats and the petals dance and shimmer with light. Detail, approximately 3:4. PHOTO BY LINDA LIGON.

PLATE VIII. *Drawloom Nishiki.* Japan, 19th century. A fragment of Japanese brocade depicting the type of loom upon which it was woven. Colors: black, dark blue, yellow and white on a blue ground. COURTESY OF THE METROPOLITAN MUSEUM OF ART, GIFT OF MR. AND MRS. H.O. HAVEMEYER, 1896.

Chapter 4

FIBER & FORM

ilk is a unique fiber: in how it looks, in how it feels and, for the textile artist, in how it works.

It is a fiber of many forms: one is the fine, shimmering, gossamer thread that first comes to mind. Silk is also spun into heavy, fat yarns, light, fluffy yarns, textured lumpy and bumpy yarns, and dense, weighty, drapey yarns.

Fiber lengths of silk yarns range from half an inch to continuous filaments almost half a mile long. The size of the yarn can range from the finest possible thread, that reeled from two cocoons, to fat yarns a quarter inch or more in diameter. The twist of the yarn can be none at all for some reeled yarns, to over a hundred turns per inch for crêpe yarns. Silk fabrics come in all combinations of these yarns, and commonly in about a dozen main weave types. Silk fiber for hand spinning has an equal range: from cloud-like, very short-fibered noil, to the long-fibered "caps". It is even possible to obtain, or raise, cocoons and reel the silk.

For the textile craftsman, yarn, fiber and fabric are a substantial investment, whether we buy it for a project in mind now or build a piece around it later. To makes the best use of a yarn/fiber/fabric, its qualities must be fully understood before work begins. Otherwise there is the possibility of warps that break again and again, or fantastic garments that took months to knit, weave or sew, and which wear out too quickly; conversely, of using a very expensive yarn/fabric for a piece that could have been done with something less costly yet better suited to the purpose.

Appearance & Quality

The first thing one notices about a silk is its appearance. This always remains its most important attraction, whatever its structure and usefulness. With silk, appearances are not that deceptive. It is often possible to judge the important qualities of a yarn from how it looks. Tests become confirmation. It is harder to judge a yarn once it is woven into fabric, so the two yarns, warp and weft, in a fabric should always be examined before any assumption is made about the fabric's quality.

The relationship between appearance and quality in a silk has two aspects. The first is that a beautiful appearance is one of the desirable qualities of silk. The second considers quality as strength and durability. The appearance of a yarn is determined by its constituent fibers and the type of spin. These are the same variables that determine its strength and durability. Long parallel fibers are needed for a yarn to appear lustrous; long fibers give inherent strength. Very short fibers show little balls of tangles (called noils) that decrease a yarn's luster; very short fibers spin a weak yarn.

Without careful examination the only other guides to quality are cost and feel. Cost is not terribly reliable. Silk prices are often well related to quality, perhaps because silk is bought mostly by people who've sought it out and are somewhat familiar with quality variations. But there are always exceptions as many factors govern retail pricing; it is better to check out quality and not rely on price. Besides, how would you know a real bargain if you couldn't determine quality independent of price? Note that tussah, wild silk is generally a little less expensive than cultivated white silk, other factors being equal.

Hand & Drape

The feel of a yarn or fabric is as important as its appearance. Smooth it on your cheek: is it soft, smooth, pleasingly textured? Squeeze up a handful: does it feel limp or resilient? Resiliency is called "body". A lack of body can mean damaged fibers, reprocessed silk, or very short fibers of poor quality. Body can be artifically increased by sizing (starching), or by scroping, the process that makes silk very rustly. Silk without body is tactily uninteresting, and I would avoid it.

The hand and drape of a yarn or fabric is important to its use. But unless one has a bag of fiber, skeins of yarn, or yards of fabric to feel, these qualities can be hard to judge. Try to feel the silk under question as much as possible anyway. Slubby yarns and fabrics look and feel relatively rough. Smoothness is needed for a "silky" feel. Does the amount of silk feel heavy and dense? Dense, heavy yarns drape well. Or does the silk feel light, fluffy, lofty? Some weaves require a lofty (compressible) yarn for best effect, for instance the pattern weft in overshot. Others would be smothered by a lofty yarn, for instance traditional gauze, a weave developed for the smoothest, slipperiest silk yarns. If not held in place by gauze crossings, very smooth, slippery silks need a close sett and tight beat to weave a sturdy fabric.

Some examples of the unique
Hand & Drape of Silk:

Square cut garments like the kimono, that mold themselves to the grace of the wearer.

Saris — lengths of fabric arranged in flowing folds.

To wear a silk sari is like swimming in gossamer and air: effortless motion.

Scarves — from the triangularly folded square to the long fluttering rectangle.

And on the heavier side:

Velvets, brocades and thick contemporary handwovens — even the heaviest silks are soft, supple and lightweight.

A fabric woven of markedly different warp and weft will drape differently length-wise or cross-ways, as folds will form more easily across the softer or thinner yarn. In most fabrics the warp is stiffer, but when it is much finer than the weft, the drape could be the other way. Check the fabric for wrinkle resistance by crumpling it and shaking it out. If the wrinkles stay in, the fabric will wrinkle when worn. Then consider that old rule which says that the closer the warp and weft are to being the same size yarns, the longer the whole fabric will wear.

Testing Silks for Their Qualities — Strength & Elasticity

The first thing to test is strength and elasticity. Take a length of yarn and pull it. Feel how elastic it is, how springy, how far it will stretch. Pull until it breaks. Was that too easy or very hard? A fine yarn will break easier than a heavy, so judge its strength relative to its size. Doubling or trebling a fine yarn will give a better feel for how strong it would be under use for warp, etc. Sizing can strengthen a warp to some extent, but mostly sizing is used to keep loose spun and singles yarns from fraying where the fraying would make them weak.

To Test A Fabric's Yarns . . .
unravel lengths of both warp (length-ways) and weft (selvedge to selvedge) yarns, and examine each. For fabric on bolts, test the weft, which is what unravels at the cut edge, and just look as carefully as possible at the warp.

For Yarn . . .
if you are in a shop with an inviolable skein, hunt till you find the skein tie. There is usually an inch or so extra yarn there, to give some idea of fiber quality and length. As with small fabric *swatches*, examine and test as much as is possible.

For Spinning Fiber
you might like to spin up a bit and test it as "your" yarn.

The best yarn for warp, and the best for knitting, is elastic as well as strong. The more harness manipulation the warp has to undergo, the more elasticity is important. Your experience in breaking the yarn is the best guide: did it spring back after stretching? did it stretch before breaking? did it stretch a lot?

Check fabric directly for stretchiness. Tug in both directions and on the bias. Most fabrics will stretch more in the warp direction (lengthwise) because the warp yarns need to be elastic for weaving. Crêpe fabrics may have a very tightly twisted and stretchy weft, too. The resiliency of the fabric to being stretched out of shape is shown by bias pulling. A resilient fabric will spring right back.

Loosely woven silks have a greater tendency to pull out of shape than do tightly woven ones. There is also a tendency for the threads to pull out of the weave, especially when the fabric is wet. Such a fabric may not stand dyeing, or perhaps even washing, well, especially at seams. Run the fabric hard between pinched fingers to see if threads are pulled out of place. Check this in both directions. If threads pull out of place easily, this "defect" could be used to create interesting moiré-like effects, but for general use, consider such fabric with caution. Holding the fabric to the light will also display the closeness of the weave.

Fiber Quality

What is the character of the individual fibers? Are they coarse or fine? Tussah fibers are noticeably coarser than cultivated silk. They are correspondingly more durable. Cultivated silk will make a lighter, more gossamer fabric, and its hand is the softest.

Note that a white-colored silk could be a bleached tussah, and a dyed silk could be either wild or cultivated fiber. And a yarn without much luster or sparkles may not be fully degummed. (A good way to check this is to try degumming a bit.) Fully degummed silk is softer, more lustrous and sparkly than a silk with some or all of its gum retained. But the gum has value as protection to the fiber, and its dull, soft luster is preferred for some effects.

Fiber Length

The length of the fibers of which a yarn is spun contributes to its character, durability and usefulness. Other important variables are the individual fibers' diameter and strength, the uniformity of fibers in the yarn, and the spin of the yarn. Testing for fiber length displays the individual fibers, and makes it easy to see the other qualities.

Untwist one end of the yarn for 6"-8". With a plied yarn you'll have to untwist it twice: first untwist the plying, then separate the strands and untwist one of them (or both, if they are different). When the fibers are parallel, start pulling out bits of fibers. First pull out the cut fibers at the end of the yarn, then pinch the fibers just far enough in from the fluffy tip that you've got a full yarn-diameter of them. Pull gently. If nothing happens, don't force it. It means the yarn is not untwisted parallel enough, the fibers are longer than the amount that was untwisted, or it is possible you have a continuous fiber, reeled silk yarn, or a continuous fiber handspun yarn.

Many silk fabrics are woven of reeled silk, and sewing thread is usually reeled silk, but handweaving yarns are very rarely reeled silk. The easiest way to assess if a yarn is reeled silk is to untwist an area of it, either at the end or in the middle, and pull it out into a fan or lozenge. If the yarn is reeled silk, no ends will show; all the fibers will open out into a webby net.

Continuous fibered handspun yarns are pulled directly from cocoons. They are fluffier than reeled silk because the fibers are not smoothly parallel and, as well, some fibers will have been broken during spinning. Usually spun rather thickly, drawn-out yarns can be quite fine. They look decidedly like spun silk, but because the fiber is functionally continuous, it is not possible to pull out bits of staple.

If, however, it does seem the yarn is staple spun silk, continue to untwist it, and be sure to untwist until the fibers are parallel. Good natural light helps. Keep at it until you can pull out a pinch of fibers. Repeat the untwisting and pulling until you have three or four pulled out bits. They should all be about the same size. If they are not, you have probably pulled out more than one fiber cluster. Check by pulling out only the longest fibers from the longer bits. It may mean you've broken some longer fibers as you pulled bits out.

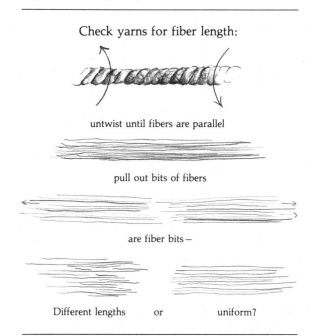

Check yarns for fiber length:

untwist until fibers are parallel

pull out bits of fibers

are fiber bits —

Different lengths   or   uniform?

Check the pinches for uniformity by pulling them apart. A bit whose fibers may at first appear to vary from 3"-5" may actually be of uniformly 4" fibers. Uniform fiber length gives a sleeker, denser yarn. If tightly twisted, such a yarn will feel heavy for silk. This heaviness makes it drape and hang well, but could be a disadvantage if you wanted silk for lightweight bulkiness.

The lower limit for a serviceable warp is a fiber length of 1". That is, if the fiber length of a yarn is 1" or more, it could be used for warp. However, if the fiber length is less than 2", the yarn will need a very tight twist or sizing to hold it together. It is safest to choose warp yarns from those whose staple is 3" or more, and which have a good twist or are plied. This would also hold for yarns chosen for knitting. Otherwise, use your judgment on the breaking test and decide if you want to chance some breakage in weaving.

Most spun silk yarns, except noil and reprocessed silk, have a staple length between 2"-6". Evidently the upper limit for machine spinning is 12". Longer staple is too difficult to handle by machine but is available for handspinning.

Noil

Noil is a very important class of silk with many unique properties. It is the very short fibers left after the longer staple silk has been combed out. It consists of smooth fibers 1" and shorter, mixed with little tangled balls of fiber. Because of the very short fibres, noil yarns are weak and inelastic. They don't make good warp, although some weavers do use it. Finer noil yarns may be too weak for high speed bobbin winding, although otherwise they would make good weft. Under use, noil wears out relatively quickly, as the very short fibers disintegrate more rapidly than do intact long fibers. However, noil fabrics have several unique characteristics that make them very popular.

The necessary tight twist of a noil yarn obscures the silk luster, as do the little balls of tangled fiber. They make a noil yarn or fabric always somewhat rough textured. A good quality noil yarn will have a visually unusual combination of a slight, lurking luster, and sparkling highlights, on a matte (rough, granular) surface. A good bleached noil will have a visual texture like clouds: not shiny, but lustrous in a glowing, delicate way. It is a good medium for color. Watch out for poor quality noil which is dull and lifeless, both visually and to the hand, and which may in fact be reprocessed silk.

Unbleached, cultivated silk noil usually has small black flecks appearing throughout. These flecks are the crumbled remains of the chrysalis, that horn-like envelope that actually encloses the transforming silk caterpillar inside the cocoon. The fiber near the chrysalis, spun by the spent worm, is too weak to reel. It becomes the source of most of the fine tangled cardings that make the noil. Unbleached noil is a light tan color due to the oils coming from the chrysalis. Silkworm chrysalids are so oily that they are ground and the oils extracted. The residue silk-chrysalis-meal is used as a high-protein food supplement. (No waste.)

Because the natural tan color of noil isn't always as desirable as pure white, and as the oil can interfere with dyeing, noil is sometimes bleached. Bleached noil is very attractive, and it dyes brilliantly. Bleaching seems to increase silk's affinity for dyestuffs, and the bright, glowing white-white base gives an extraordinary brightness to the colors. The textured noil surface doesn't wash out color, as happens with a highly lustrous silk where the surface luster lightens the apparent color. (This is true, in degrees, of any textured silk yarn or fabric, velvet being the extreme for color depth and richness.)

Tussah noil is stronger than white silk noil. The straight

fibers are often longer, and individually stronger. Tussah noil is usually the combings out from the whole cocoons; the white noil comes mostly from the inner part of the cocoon, where the fiber is thinner and more delicate. Tussah noil yarns are often used as warp in handweaving and present no handling problem as long as they have a good twist.

Often, a noil fiber, yarn or fabric is labeled as such, but not always. As you examine any noil, you will notice the characteristic tangled balls that formed when the short fibers were being carded. Usually you can see these little balls on the surface of the yarn, without pulling it apart. They are one of the first things to look for, in examining a yarn, as they are an indicator of short fibers.

Reprocessed Silk

If the fibers of a silk yarn appear very non-uniform, the yarn may be spun from reprocessed silk. Silk waste from any source may be used including thrums and floor sweepings from weaving mills, and fabric wastage from garment cutting. The yarn or fabric is pulled apart to free the fibers which are then carded and spun like noil. There isn't any uniformity to the fibers in the resulting yarn since fibers from all sources are spun together. In fact, you can sometimes find that some of the constituent "fibers" are really bits of fine yarn.

Reprocessed silk yarns typically appear to have been dyed speckled. This comes about because some of the waste fibers were from dyed yarns. Rather than worry about it the spinner may mix everything together, then lightly over-dye the final yarn. The result is the speckled appearance. It's an unusual and attractive texture.

Aspects of SPIN

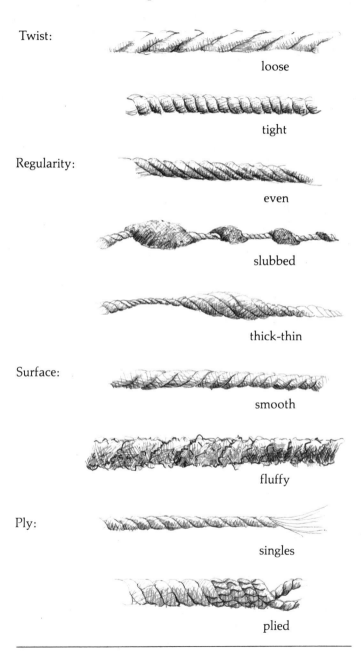

Twist:

loose

tight

Regularity:

even

slubbed

thick-thin

Surface:

smooth

fluffy

Ply:

singles

plied

Table of Silk Yarns by Fiber Length

Reeled, *Continuous filament* — smooth, sleek, almost translucent. Twist may be very tight, for warp and crêpe yarns, to almost non-existent. Very strong and elastic, with elasticity increased by tight twist.

Handspun, *continuous fibers,* pulled from cocoons — usually thickish, with a medium twist, but may be very fine. Softer and rounder yarns than reeled silk. Strong, because fiber is functionally continuous. Often sized for easier handling.

Cut Fibers —

long (3"-6"), and *combed* — smooth spun, lustrous and sleek. Dense and heavy if tightly twisted. Strong.

medium (2"-3"), *combed* — smooth spun but softer, fluffier yarns than the longer staple. In tussahs, often matte, because not fully degummed. Not strong unless tightly twisted; often used as weft with longer staple warp.

medium (2"-3"), *carded* — rough spun, with a tight twist or slubby, nubbly texture. Less lustrous but often more sparkly than combed fibers. Interesting rough textures. Remarkably strong and elastic if tightly twisted or plied.

noil — very short fibers (½"-1") and little tangle-balls of fiber. Usually tightly spun and matte. Natural white silk noil (sometimes called "raw silk") has a characteristic off-white color and little black specks of chrysalid remains in it. Soft hand. Generally weak yarns with little elasticity.

reprocessed silk — very irregular fiber content, usually looks "speckled". Soft, often too soft, with a limp hand. Weak yarns with little elasticity, unless some longer fiber has been spun in.

Chapter 5

TWIST, PLY & FUNCTION

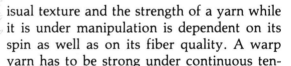isual texture and the strength of a yarn while it is under manipulation is dependent on its spin as well as on its fiber quality. A warp yarn has to be strong under continuous tensions, a knitting yarn and an embroidery thread have to withstand tension and abrasion (pulling through cloth). A yarn for hand dyeing has to be cohesive when wet and is more easily handled if it is smooth surfaced. These strengths are governed by spin as much as by fiber.

The twist of the yarns in a fabric plays a good part in its durability, especially in a loosely woven fabric. A tight twist gives strength to short fibers. A tight twist can also give elasticity to a yarn/fabric, as with crêpes.

The twist of a yarn has a great effect on its visual texture and on its hand. A soft twist, showing the fibers almost parallel, will have a high luster, and it will feel smooth and soft. A tight twist breaks up the luster. It also makes a rounded, substantial yarn. Nubbly or thick-and-thin spins add interesting tactile and visual irregularities.

Elasticity & Strength

The basic principle of yarn construction is that twist is what keeps the yarn together. It is the twist which turns a loose aggregate of fibers into a cohesive yarn. The amount of twist given to the fibers affects the strength and elasticity of the resulting yarn as much as does its fiber make-up. In a loose twist yarn the fibers lie relatively parallel to the length of the yarn. In a tight twist yarn they lie at a pronounced angle. An individual fiber may circle the yarn many times, so the "catchiness" of the fiber has more to hold on to as each fiber crosses many others. Additionally, the encircling fibers hold the yarn together by the tension of their individual elasticity.

The tension of the encircling fibers accounts for the added strength that a tight twist gives to a yarn. Also added is elasticity because in a tight twist yarn the transverse elasticity of the fiber is brought into use. As the yarn is pulled lengthwise, the fibers are crushed transversely as well as pulled along their length. As the silk fiber is very resilient to crushing, the transverse elasticity helps the yarn spring back. In fact, this transverse elasticity of the fiber is more important to the elasticity of a silk yarn than is the fiber's longitudinal elasticity. It is the reason that organzine — tightly twisted and plied, reeled silk yarn — is synonymous with warp silk.

This points to an advantage of handspun yarns. Since handspinning proceeds with more tension on the fibers while they're being twisted, the resulting yarn is stronger than a comparable machine spun yarn. The extra tension holds it together well. The additional tension also makes a handspun yarn especially elastic and gives it a substantial, springy body and hand.

Sparkles & Luster

The spin greatly affects the visual texture of a yarn. A smooth, loose twist displays silk's luster, a very tight twist will obscure luster, but it may display the sparkles. The sparkles of the silk fiber come from any irregularities in its surface. A reeled yarn is very regular and not very sparkly. Delicate sparkles due to small irregularities in the extruded fiber surface are visible, especially in sunlight; but what is striking about reeled silk is its translucent luster. Sparkles are created wherever the fiber is bent; light strikes the minute surfaces created by the bends and crinkles, and is reflected back as though each surface were a little mirror. There is a small prismatic, rainbow effect, most noticeable in sunlight. The reflected light dances and sparkles: diamonds and pearls. The sparkles are brought out by twisting and by weaving, twining or otherwise bending the yarn's fibers.

Another aspect of luster vs. sparkles lies on the yarn's surface. There are always cut ends of fiber sticking out of a spun yarn. These are sometimes singed off, a process known as "gassing". The yarn is run quickly through a small flame, just hot enough to burn the loose ends but not affect the dense yarn. This gives a smooth surface and improves luster. But on a yarn which has not been singed, each cut end sticking out is another sparkle. A yarn, smooth spun of long, parallel fibers, given a medium twist and not singed, can have high sparkle over high luster.

This visual texture can also be effected by hand dyeing a lustrous but short fibered singles yarn. Some surface matting is inevitable, and each mat is a swarm of sparkles.

Ply

Twist is what keeps a yarn together. Ply is important along with twist because ply helps to retain a twist. A single strand of yarn tends to untwist. While a loose spun singles may seem strong when pulled, under long periods of tension the fibers will tend to slip past each other, and the yarn may pull apart. However, in a plied yarn under tension, the untwisting of the ply will just twist up the component singles tighter, so the yarn loses no strength.

On the other hand, a very tight twist singles may have enough excess twist that tension does not affect its strength. If the fibers are long enough, it will be both strong and very elastic. This yarn would be fine for warp, for instance, and gives an entirely different texture than does a plied warp.

Plied yarns may be tightly or loosely twisted, either in

their singles, or in the ply. Each combination gives a slightly different texture. A tightly twisted and tightly two- or three-plied yarn has a rounded pebbly look. Increase the number of strands to four or five and the pebbly effect is lost: the aggregate surface is smoooother, although the yarn is just as dense and round. A loosely twisted and plied yarn may be hard to distinguish from a singles, but it will still have the added strength due to plying.

With a loose twist yarn, fiber length becomes very important to stretch, durability, cohesiveness, etc. If the fibers are short, the loose twist yarn will fray, plied or not. This tendency to fray can be used to texture the surface of the yarn: it can be brushed, fluffed out, or matted to accent silk's sparkles.

PLYING

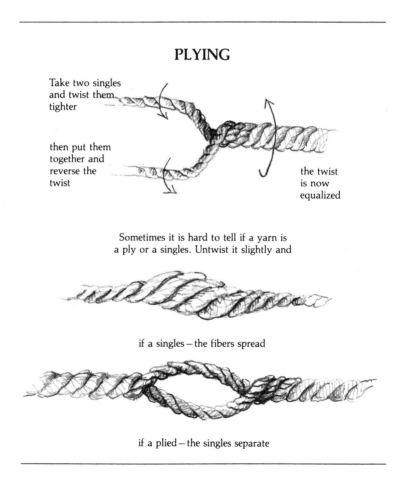

Take two singles and twist them tighter

then put them together and reverse the twist

the twist is now equalized

Sometimes it is hard to tell if a yarn is a ply or a singles. Untwist it slightly and

if a singles — the fibers spread

if a plied — the singles separate

Choosing Yarns

A yarn's twist, its ply, and its fiber length: three aspects which work together to form a yarn. They determine its character and usefulness, and must always be considered together.

For instance, to answer the frequent question: what yarn is best for warp? It's easy enough to say: this cord-like yarn is "best". It is "best" because it is strong, heavy, elastic and will never break or fray. What gives it those qualities? It is long staple, tightly twisted and plied, and it is so large diametered it's impossible to break.

But who wants to be restricted to only "the best" warp? What other yarns will work for warp? or for knitting? or to embroider with? What are the qualities to look for?

Strength and elasticity are empiric qualities, they can be tested for by breaking the yarn. The yarn's twist, ply and fiber component are the aspects of its construction which, working together, determine such empiric qualities as strength, elasticity, resistance to fraying, shedding or matting, as well as the yarn's hand and its visual character—not just now, but also five, ten or fifty years from now. By carefully examining a yarn, its construction can be confirmed, and the empiric qualities deduced. Then a careful choice can be made to match a yarn to its intended use.

Knitting

Yarns for knitting have similarities to yarns for warp. Any kind of fancy pattern knitting puts stress on single strands for the lifetime of the piece, especially at "yarn over" openings. The interlacings of a knit aren't as dense as those of a woven fabric where the multiple crossings meld the yarns together; knitting doesn't strengthen its component yarns the way weaving does. A yarn for knitting, whether smooth and dense or light and fluffy, has to have inherent strength.

The twist and ply of the yarn, besides contributing strength, influence the texture of the knit. A tight singles will tend to make a very tight, elastic and stretchy fabric. A plied yarn will give textures closest to the standard wool knitting yarns. A loose singles will tend to mesh down into a flat, texturally smooth surface. This surface could be made fluffy with

Silk yarns for
Warp and Knitting

Best: fiber length 2″ or more,
smooth spun
plied,
tight twist

Very Good: fiber length 2″ or more,
plied,
medium twist

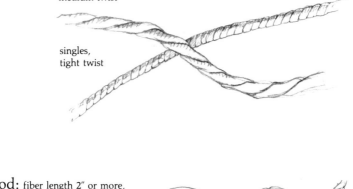

singles,
tight twist

Good: fiber length 2″ or more,
singles or plied,
with slubs or
thick-thin

singles,
medium twist

Other silk yarns can be used for warp if they are sized or handled
carefully.

the fiber displayed rather than the knit: e.g., brushed into a soft shag.

A tightly twisted yarn, singles or plied, is usually preferred if the weave or knit is loose and open. Otherwise the texture of the weave/knit is lost in the loose, opened out yarn. Besides, loosely incorporated fibers invite catching, pulling and breaking, all disastrous to a loose weave or knit.

Crochet

Crochet has a much denser interlacing than knitting. It is based on a looped chain totaling three strands in diameter. Attachments (interlacings) are always a double strand (a loop). So it is reasonable to use more delicate yarns than would be best for knitting. A thick noil singles, for instance, gives an interesting texture. Warp type yarns, especially a tight twist singles or a cord, work especially well for filet lace.

Lace

Bobbin lace and macramé require warp type yarns. Traditionally, tightly twisted and regular cords are used. For contemporary work any strong yarn can be used. A weak yarn can be used if it is combined with a strong yarn: for instance, a heavy noil loosely twisted on a thin, strong warp silk. The stronger thread should be manipulated to take the stresses in the finished piece. (See boucléd yarns, pages 70-71.)

Weft

Weft yarns do not usually need the strength of warp yarns. However, if the weave is complex, especially if it has long floats, the fiber length of the weft and its twist and ply are important to consider. If the fiber length of a yarn is only two times the float length of the weave, almost half the fibers will not bridge the whole float. They will tend to work out of the yarn, and the float will felt. So for weaves like overshot the pattern weft should have a good long staple, unless you plan to brush out the floats for a shag effect.

The tendency for a very short fibered yarn to felt at floats can be held in check by a very tight twist. But a tight twist singles will, on washing, shrink up any place it can: for instance in long weaving floats! This is the principle of crêpes — tight twist singles woven with lots of space between, to give them room to shrink and krinkle. Pre-shrink (page 124) such a yarn before weaving if a crêped effect is not wanted. Or use a plied yarn instead.

Pile

Yarns for pile fabrics should be chosen with care. One wants a tightly twisted and plied yarn for a long-pile, rya effect. But a loose, parallel twist is necessary for knotted Oriental carpets or for velvet/plush where the pile effect is of fibers, not of yarns. It doesn't matter in this case if the yarn is a singles or plied, but long fiber is essential. The fiber should be several times longer than the pile, or too many short ends will brush out when the pile is cut and brushed.

Tussah is the traditional silk used for pile because it is thicker and therefore stronger than white silk. It is also slightly more resilient and gives good body to a carpet. Besides, if the yarn is going to be cut anyway, a long staple spun silk is just as good as a continuous filament.

Cut pile is especially effective for color; the cut ends look very deep.

Embroidery

In embroidery, two main spins are used for two different visual effects. Soft, loosely twisted *floss* displays silk's luster, especially in large areas of satin stitch. It's also used for the various cross stitches. It forms a flat surface; it spreads out and covers well. Almost any loosely twisted two-ply or even a singles can be used this way.

Tightly twisted and plied *cord*, also called cordonnet and twist, is especially good for chain stitch, buttonhole stitch and any looped or feathered stitch. The cabled texture of the cord is important to these.

Another silk used for embroidery is the very fine thread used for *couching*. Metal threads are usually couched with very fine silk in a matching color. Sometimes a constrasting color is used, stitched to form its own pattern across the couched area. Heavy cord silk can be couched, for outlines or to cover very large areas. This is especially effective if the silk cord is slightly variegated in shade. Couching thread is usually a fine, medium-twist two-ply; sewing silk can be used.

All three types used for embroidery should be as long fibered as possible, with reeled silk the ideal. For traditional work the yarn should be smooth, regular and very strong. For contemporary work, threads need to be strong enough to be pulled through the backing fabric, if they are to be stitched. Any yarn can be couched; this can be used both for quick work and for varied textures.

Sewing Silk

That silk yarn which is most widely used is silk sewing thread. It is fine, strong reeled silk. It can be used to weave with; the fabric will come off the loom very stiff, but will soften up. It must be sett and beat very tight because it is a very slippery thread. It would be ideal for gauze.

Silk fabric should always be sewn with silk thread. Only silk thread has the elasticity necessary to go with silk fabric.

American sewing silk is designed for machine sewing. It is a simple three-ply thread, and the stripping action when it is pulled through cloth in hand sewing causes it to untwist. This makes it difficult to use a double strand as it twists and kinks. A single strand, though, tends to slip out of the needle. To prevent this, ply the needle end of the thread:

After threading the needle, hold the needle end of the thread between thumb and first joint of the right hand. In the left hand hold the thread at an equal distance on the other side of the needle.

Roll the end in the right hand along the finger towards its tip. This will twist up the yarn. Move hands together: the needle pirouettes and the thread plies itself. This secures the thread so it doesn't slip out. To use a double strand without its kinking, loosely ply the whole length of the thread.

Direct spinning from opened-out cocoons, using a light-weight drop spindle. The right hand pulls out a long draw, releases the yarn to let the twist run up, then begins the next draw from the point where the twist stopped. The illustration shows the hands at the beginning of the draw. By the end of the draw the hands are about two feet apart.

Chapter 6

HANDSPINNING

andspun yarn is as different from machine spun as spun silk is from reeled. There is nothing like the substantial loft, the resilient hand and the natural elasticity of a handspun yarn. Fabrics made of handspun have a life in them: they last forever, and have no need of such modern inventions as irons to look and wear superbly.

Elaborate spinning equipment isn't necessary. A simple spindle can be made from a piece of wood and a large bead. Spindle spinning goes slower than wheel spinning; this makes it an ideal process to begin with.

There are at least two excellent spinning books whose techniques are applicable to silk. Elsie Davenport's *Your Handspinning* and Bette Hochberg's *A Handspinner's Handbook* are both basic and easy to read. Their approaches are different: Davenport is very clear on the worsted, woolen and line linen (distaff) methods, which are all techniques applicable to silk;

Bette Hochberg's approach is less formal, and she gives specific recommendations for silk fiber in some of its forms currently available to the handspinner.

Silk fibers for spinning come in a bewildering array; in fact, it's hard to imagine a greater variety: from fluffy masses of very short fibered noils, to sleek, combed "tops", to the continuous-fibered "caps". One can even spin directly from cocoons. Each form requires only slightly different spinning techniques yet gives radically different types of yarns. Linen techniques can apply to the caps, worsted techniques to combed and carded rovings, and cotton techniques to the noils.

A Silk Bouclé

Designing with commercially spun yarn is a good way to start: change the twist from tight to loose or loose to tight, ply a yarn (pages 61-62), or construct a silk bouclé.

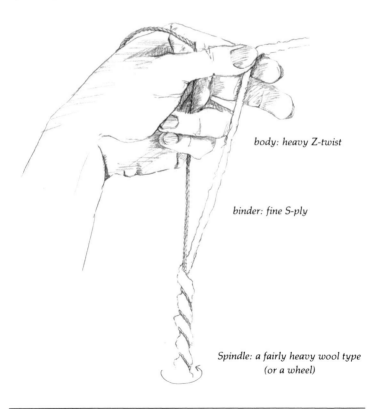

body: heavy Z-twist

binder: fine S-ply

*Spindle: a fairly heavy wool type
(or a wheel)*

Silk bouclés are very distinctive. To make a bouclé simply ply a heavy yarn with a fine yarn. Hold the fine yarn under tension and let the heavy yarn feed in at an angle. The heavy yarn makes the knobbles of the bouclé, with the fine yarn acting as binder. For strength, always twist the fine yarn tighter. If the heavy yarn also twists tighter, then the bouclé will be knubbly. If instead the heavy yarn untwists slightly during the plying, the bouclé will be soft and fluffy. For more elaborate bouclés, re-ply this simple bouclé with another fine yarn. Mix sizes, twists and colors; the possibilities are endless.

Degummed Cocoons

Cocoons are the start of it all. What can be done with them is unlimited. They can be reeled. They can be opened out and spun directly. They can be pulled out into flakes, caps or rovings to be spun, or they can be cut, carded and then spun.

Direct spinning from degummed cocoons is the classic form for handspun silk. In fact, there is no easier fiber to spin. The secret is that the fibers are continuous.

The cocoons must first be degummed (page 76). Then "poof" them out slightly: grasp the cocoon with forefinger and thumb of both hands and use many short, sharp tugs to start the opening out process. Change positions slightly after each tug and be sure to pinch all the way to the center of the cocoon, otherwise only the outer layers will be opened out. Remove the chrysalis when the puff is about three inches in diameter, then you may spin directly — just begin pulling out a thread — or you may first pull it out into a long roving.

Cocoons may be cut up the middle and the fiber carded for spinning. For a perfectly white yarn, cut them and remove the chrysalis before degumming. The crysalis' oils stain the innermost fiber a pale yellow if it is left in during degumming.

Cocoons may also be spun raw. Soak them in warm water just to soften, and then just begin pulling out fibers from one end — the unopened end, in the case the moth has emerged. This makes a stiff raw silk yarn, but it will soften on wearing and it will wear forever *(Barbara Flemming)*.

Yarns from pulled-out cocoons are very strong — because the fiber is functionally continuous. By the roving method they can be spun into a very regular yarn, dense and substantial whether fine in diameter or thick. But the most distinctive form is the fine yarn of minimal twist that is so light and fluffy it feels like a butterfly could carry it away. It is achieved through direct spinning of the opened out cocoons, or by spinning caps placed on a distaff.

This is the classic form for silk wadding. The cocoons are pulled out into a square by catching each corner on pegs or nails. The square can be spun directly or it can be pulled out into a roving first.

Mawata can be made from the unreelable center of cocoons. After reeling as much as possible, take a cocoon from the hot water. As soon as it is cool enough to handle pull it apart slightly and remove the pupa. Take four together and pull out into a square *(Jean Case)*. This center-of-cocoon fiber is especially fine, delicate and soft.

A DEFINITION:
DRAWING means pulling out the fibers so that they are under linear tension as they are being twisted.

Silk Caps

Caps are degummed cocoons which have been pulled out and over a cap-shaped form. They can be spun as described for cocoons. If they are large caps they can be placed over a distaff for some fast, efficient and very enjoyable spinning.

The caps come all wadded up. Take one and shake it lightly. Sometimes this reveals the original domed "cap" shape. Usually the caps have been a little roughly handled and the cap shape deformed. In any case, edges to the mass will soon become distinguishable. Lay it on a table and gently pull-tease it out, working around the edges.

Eventually the domed cap shape will be clear. Very gently work the shape out a bit more. When most of the pressed-in folds are opened out, the cap will be a dome about two feet in diameter. Lay it down and examine the edges. Layers will be apparent. Slowly separate these by working around the outside edge, towards the center. Avoid tearing holes in the thin web of each layer, although some holes seem inevitable. Usually each 1 ounce cap divides into four ¼ ounce layers.

Choose the best looking one and slip it over a swift-turned-distaff. An umbrella swift made into a distaff is better than a real linen distaff because it is wider, and the diameter can be changed as the cap is spun up. Set the swift *vertical* and drape a smooth cloth over the cage. Then lay on the silk. Arrange it evenly: the swift should be moved out until the cap hangs down the sides about 8"-10". Tease open those places where the fiber is matted together, or they will interfere with drawing out.

I sit with distaff on the left and wheel at the right, with the wheel as far away as it can be and still be treadled. To start, pull down a bit from the cap edge, twist slightly, and begin to pull out a long draw triangle. *Tie* the twisted end to the lead-in cord. Begin to treadle, and with the right hand leading, let the twist run up the fibers of the drawn out triangle. The right hand is now almost up to the distaff. Pinch the forming thread to stop the twist, and pull out a new draw-triangle by moving the right hand back to the wheel orifice. This movement is also the winding up of the yarn just twisted.

The left hand's purpose is to keep the drawing out of fibers smooth and regular. It must occasionally pull downwards to open out mats of fibers, especially at the lower edge of the cap, and must attend to moving around the cap a little with each draw. The action is smooth: the right arm sweeps back and forth, rhythmically drawing out and twisting yard-long lengths of thread. In the spinning of the whole cap, only a few stops are needed to adjust the cap or draw-out place, or to move the yarn on the wind-in hooks.

There is another quick and easy way to spin these caps, especially good for those layers that are very torn, and for spindle spinning. With both fists inside, simply pull out the cap layer, as though it were strudel, into a long roving. Pull out the roving further into a fluffy sliver about 1" in diameter and wrap it around a horizontally attached swift or a distaff. Spin directly from the sliver. It is easy to draw out about a 1 foot-long triangle.

One thing to note about spinning this cap silk in distinction to spinning other fiber-forms of silk: you mustn't be too delicate. Be assertive in drawing out. The reason is that the fibers are not cut. One must break some of the fibers or drawing out would not be possible. So the yarn is not really continuous filament in the reeled silk sense, but each fiber will be many yards long before it gets broken in the drawing out.

Cut Fiber

Cut silk fibers, combed or carded in preparation for machine spinning, can also be handspun. *Combed* fibers spin a smooth, lustrous yarn; *carded* fibers spin a slightly slubby yarn, less lustrous but more textural. With combed fibers, the longer the staple the easier to spin and the more lustrous and regular the yarn. *Combed tussah* is more easily spun than *combed white* because it is not quite so slippery. *Carded* silk contains varying lengths of fibers and usually some noils (tangles) as well. Thus, it isn't as smooth and slippery as combed silk and may prove easier to spin.

It is usual to try to spin cut silk fibers as one would wool or mohair. This proves difficult because silk does not have wool's crimp, scales and inherent catchiness. The one-handed self-drawing method is the easy way to spin cut silk. It takes advantage of silk's smooth slipperiness. It works well for all the cut-fiber forms of silk.

Take a small handful of parallel fibers. Hold them as in the drawing. To begin, pinch out a triangle from the center. Attach it to the lead cord, begin to treadle and let the spin run up into the triangle. Hold the fiber securely, but not too tightly, and slowly draw the hand away. Move only as fast as the twist continues to run up the emerging yarn into the handful of fibers. It is the twist itself which draws out the fibers.

One handed self-draw spinning of long staple (7″) combed tussah.

A fluffy mass of noil being spun by the one handed self-draw method. A light fluffing of the fiber is the only preparation. Easy to spin, although the yarn is not easily made regular.

When you get the hang of it, adjust the tension tighter so that you can draw out firmly against it and so the yarn has no trouble winding on. Soon you'll be treadling as fast as you can and spinning a yarn as fine and even as the fiber allows. While the technique is a little tricky at first, it's well worth the trouble to master as it is both effortless and fast. Add a new handful of fibers before all the parallel fibers are spun, and there will be no weak joints in the yarn. I have found my right hand likes to spin a fine yarn, while my left does well for a heavier yarn.

To Degum Cocoons

"For 100 home-grown cocoons (about 1 oz):
Cut them up one side and remove the chrysalids. Use three big squirts of Ivory liquid detergent (or about a third cup of Ivory soap) *and enough water to cover twice as deep as cocoons. Simmer 1½ hours* (or until the fiber is white and no longer feels slimey with silk gum).
"Rinse in a colander with a sprayer."
— Barbara Flemming

You will want to reel (page 78) those cocoons that are reelable. Broken cocoons, double cocoons, gathered wild silk, and the unreelable center portion of reeled cocoons can all be degummed and spun.

Spindle Spinning

To spindle spin cut fibers, a lightweight drop spindle can be used, but it makes for less work and faster spinning to use a heavy wool-type or brass-whorl spindle. Support it in a bowl, on a table, or on the floor to take the weight off the fibers. Twirl the spindle like a top. Draw upwards from the twirling top, letting the twist from the spinning spindle run up into the fibers exactly as described for wheel spinning.

Noil

Silk noil is available either carded into tops or simply in mass. By the following method it spins easily into a soft, woolen-type "homespun" looking yarn. Make long thin rolags,

Setting the Twist

Once spun or twisted, yarn should be carefully set to preserve its greatest elasticity. Skein the yarn, moisten slightly with a sprayer, and dry under just enough tension to keep out back twisting. I like to twist up the sprinkled yarn into a relatively loose skein-twist to dry. This works better than putting it on a swift or weighting it. Very little water is needed.

Drying or steaming under a lot of tension is used on smooth spun, long staple or reeled silk yarns where a very lustrous, smooth surface, and a traditionally "silky" drape is wanted. See also under "handling of yarns", pages 131-133 and "shrinkage", page 123.

To make a skein twist

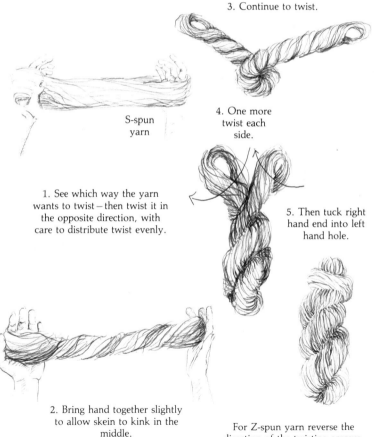

3. Continue to twist.

S-spun yarn

4. One more twist each side.

1. See which way the yarn wants to twist — then twist it in the opposite direction, with care to distribute twist evenly.

5. Then tuck right hand end into left hand hole.

2. Bring hand together slightly to allow skein to kink in the middle.

For Z-spun yarn reverse the direction of the twisting arrows.

either by carding loose noil, or by splitting tops. Then very carefully pull out the rolags into long, very delicate slivers. Compact the slivers by rolling them between palms. It is not possible to draw noil, as the fibers are too short, so spinning simply imparts twist to this long, fluffy caterpillar. Noil yarns spun this way are thickish, even, dense but compressible and surprisingly strong.

Hand-reeling Silk

Choose perfect cocoons from well-fed worms. Simmer the cocoons for 10-15 minutes to soften the gum. Go over each cocoon carefully with a toothbrush until a continuous end is found, then gather six or eight ends together and begin to reel. Watch the cocoons bobble in the hot water; if one stops it is a sign that filament has broken. Re-find the end and attach it to the thread before continuing *(Jean Case)*.

The inner portion of the cocoon will be too weak to reel. It can be pulled out or carded for spinning.

Spinning is such pleasant work
such a natural occupation

Once, nearly every woman
in the world and many a man
was a spinner

PLATE IX. A variety of silk fabrics. Reading clockwise from upper left: damask; chiffon; crêpe de chine; tussah and white noils alternating, from India; white shantung; half-raw tussah, from India; satin; China silk; heavy tussah, half-raw, from China; tussah shantung, from China (center). PHOTO BY JOE COCA.

PLATE X. *Sleeveband* (detail). China, c. 1875. Silk embroidery on silk satin. COURTESY OF THE DENVER ART MUSEUM.

PLATE XI. *Cloud Patterns.* 11″×12″. Diane Itter, USA, 1975. Knotted. Silk cord naturally dyed by Cheryl Kolander. PHOTO BY DIANE ITTER.

PLATE XII. *Man's Summer dragon robe* (detail), 1800-1825. Silk embroidery on silk gauze. COURTESY OF THE DENVER ART MUSEUM.

PLATE XIII. *Butterfly Lady.* Dixie McKinney, USA, 1978. Embroidery-embellished knit. Naturally dyed silk cord, and mercerized cotton. Sweater detail, approximately full size. PHOTO BY JOE COCA.

PLATE XIV. *Shawl.* Cheryl Kolander, USA, 1975. Plain weave silk cord with weft pattern floats and plaited fringe.

PLATE XV. *Woman's dragon robe* (detail). China, 1875-1900. Silk tapestry. COURTESY OF THE DENVER ART MUSEUM.

PLATE XVI. *Silk chenille towel.* Cheryl Kolander, USA, 1980. PHOTO BY JOE COCA.

Chapter 7

FABRICS

"In the time of swords and periwigs and full-skirted coats with flowered lappets — when gentlemen wore ruffles, and gold-laced waistcoats of paduasoy and taffeta — there lived a tailor in Gloucester.

"He sat in the window of a little shop in Westgate Street, cross-legged on a table, from morning till dark.

"All day long while the light lasted he sewed and snippeted, piecing out his satin and pompadour, and lutestring; stuffs had strange names, and were very expensive in the days of the Tailor of Gloucester."

— Beatrix Potter
The Tailor of Gloucester

---

rmure. (French: *armour; weave*). Fabric of modified or broken warp rib weave; or with small designs on a rib or twill ground. The effect is pebbly or embossed, and looks something like medieval armor made of overlapping plates. Sometimes two kinds of warp are used, alternating one then the other, end and end: S and Z twist; silk and wool; etc. This increases the pebbly effect. In any fiber, but especially shimmery in silk. Used for dresses, scarves, waistcoats, drapery. (See also *Barathea.*)

Balloon Fabric. Very fine, light and strong, plain woven silk or cotton. Made impenetrable by coating with rubber or varnish. One kind is built up of three layers of cloth set warpways, weft-ways and diagonally (on the bias) so that it will not tear or split even if pierced.

Barathea. A general name for armure-like fabrics. The pebbly weave may be broken into ribs or stripes, two colors are often used, as well as two different fibers. Also used specifically for a pebbly surfaced, broken weft rib weave.

Batiste. A fine, thin plain-weave cloth of silk, cotton, linen, rayon, etc. Sheer, lighter than challis. Named after its inventor, Baptiste Chambrai, a 13th century French weaver.

Bengaline. (From *Bengal*, India.) a heavy warp rib with silk warp and cotton, soft spun woolen or worsted weft. Only the silk warp shows, covering very rounded crosswise ribs. *Bengaline de Soie:* with silk warp and weft.

Bobbinet. Plain bobbin lace: the hexagonal mesh net used for lace grounds.

Boulting Cloth. An open mesh raw silk used for seives (bolters). The warp is a fine, hard twist organzine. The plain gauze-weave, square mesh is held in place by the silk gum. Used by flour mills and pharmacies, for printing screens in dyeworks, and for embroidery.

Bombazine. The name of several silk or half-silk twill fabrics. Usually dyed black and used for mourning. *Bombycine* is used by Cox for wild silk. In *Les Soieries d'Art* he expresses the opinion Pamphile spun "bombycine", not "soie".

Bourette, Bourrette. Yarn of silk, cotton or linen with a rough, uneven texture, spun from carded rather than combed fiber, and the fabric woven of such yarn.

Broadsilk. Technically, any silk woven wider than 18″. (Under 18″ classes it as ribbon.) Now used for a medium light-weight taffeta, usually with spun weft, used for shirts and blouses.

Lutestring — Lustring — a 17th to 19th century finely ribbed silk.
Paduasoy — Poudesoy — (from French: *pou de soie)* a rich, corded silk.

Brocade. (From *broccus,* Latin: *stitching.*) A much used term, with both specific and general meanings. In old definitions, brocade is figured silk, with the figures all or partly made of gold or silver. In contemporary use, brocading is a technique whereby figures are lain in so the figure wefts go only as far as the edge of the figure, then they turn back for the next figure pick. It is as though the brocaded figure were a small tapestry, interwoven in the cloth. There is also a "warp brocade" technique using extra, usually heavier, pattern warps that weave in only part of the fabric width. Brocade figures, whether formed by extra wefts, warps or by embroidery, are described as "raised" above the ground/surface of the cloth. "Brocade" is also now used almost interchangeably with "tapestry" or "Jacquard" to refer to any richly figured silk, usually of multiple colors.

Brocade designs may be geometric or minutely pictorial; they may cover the ground or be placed at intervals. The ground can be any weave: satin seems to have been the favorite in the West; twill is used in Japan, and in many Persian and Byzantine brocades. Sometimes pattern wefts not needed at the front are left to float across the back, making a one-sided fabric. Occasionally, to solve the problem, such long floats are simply cut away. Or the weave may be designed to incorporate the floats, either by stitching them down at intervals or by weaving them into a double-cloth backing fabric. Phillipe de LaSalle began the use of chenille wefts to give areas the effect of velvet.

Heavy brocades are used for hangings and curtains; light ones for formal dresses, robes, obis, etc. (See *nishiki* for Japanese brocades; also *broché, brocatelle, damask, jacquard, k'o ssu, lampas, samite.*)

Brocatelle. A kind of brocade with raised design. Heavy, usually all silk and used for upholstery and heavy draperies. Flemming defines as a damask with a ground weave other than satin.

Broché. Embroidery-like brocade effects using extra warps or wefts laid in by hand, or woven mechanically with a lappet device or swivel *(Watson).*

Plain Weaves

Balanced
China Silk
Habutai
Sari Silk
Taffeta

Weft Faced
Tapestry

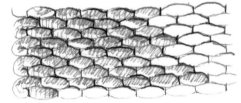

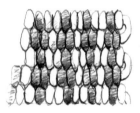

Warp Faced
one pick
per shed
Repp

Warp Faced
— several picks
per shed
Faille
Grosgrain

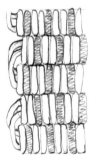

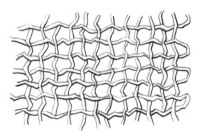

Crepes

Cachemire de soie. (French: *cashmere of silk.*) Fine twill finished to look like cashmere.

Canvas. Silk canvas is woven as habutai, but not degummed. Used by caligraphers and painters.

Challis, Challie. Originally a lightweight silk and wool fabric; now all wool or wool with cotton or rayon.

Charmeuse. A 20th century satin with semi-lustrous surface and dull back. Soft and lightweight with a good drape. Hard twist organzine warp is crossed by either schappe or hard twist crepe filling. If with former, called *satin charmeuse;* if with latter, called *crepe charmeuse.* Both distinguished by their soft hand and dull luster. Piece dyed; used for dresses.

Chenille. (French: *caterpillar.*) A velvet textured yarn, used for embroidery, fringes, carpets, bedspreads, knitting and crochet, and as a weft to give woven areas the effect of velvet.

Chiffon. (French: *rag.*) A sheer, open plain weave of hard twist raw singles both warp and weft, degummed in the piece for a very soft hand. Also called crepe georgette. As an adjective, for instance "chiffon taffeta", refers to a light weight and a soft hand.

China Silk. Originally a plain weave silk handwoven in China from hand-reeled silk that was distinguished by a beautiful natural luster. Now a plain weave silk, lightweight and lustrous, one of the staples of the hand dyer. Sometimes also called habutai, of which it is a lightweight type. Woven all silk or part rayon and commercially available in many colors. Used especially for scarves and linings. It is a fairly delicate silk with a tendency to snag if not handled with care.

Chiné, Chené. Fabrics where the design has been printed on the warp before weaving. The effect is a design slightly indistinct, or "watered". Once very popular for silk ribbons. The weave is usually plain: balanced, warp rib or crepe. The technique is attributed to China, thus the name, but is probably a western version—printed rather than tie-dyed—of Japanese *kasuri* and Indonesian *ikat.* Also called *dresden.*

Cleaning Cloth. A coarse plain or gauze weave fabric of cotton or spun silk, used for cleaning machinery. According to Watson, silk is (or was) used in cleaning woolen mills, for fire safety.

Cloth of Gold. An ancient and traditional ceremonial cloth. Round wires or flat strips of gold were used, and later, flat strips wound around a silk core. Silk became the traditional warp, and the cloth was generally woven pick and pick, silk and gold, though sometimes entirely gold.

Crepe. (from *crispus*, Latin: *curled*.) Silk crepe fabric is plain woven. The creped or crinkled effect is due to the twist of the yarns: very tight twist warp, weft, or both are used, and the sett and beat are open enough to allow the yarns to shrink up when wet-finished. This makes the crinkled or pebbly surface texture, and gives crepe a stretchy hand.

There are other ways of making crepe. *Crepe weaves* produce cloth with an irregular or broken surface using ordinary yarns. Davison gives many variations used by handweavers. Another way to produce a crepe is to use a supplemental warp that is only lightly weighted. Beating crinkles it up, somewhat like a low terry. A fourth way to make crepe is to use two dissimilar fibers or yarns which shrink differently. For instance, wild silk crossed by white silk: a sulphuric acid bath will shrink the white silk, leaving the wild to crinkle and crepe.

Plain-weave silk crepes vary in several ways: size and proportion of yarns used; whether warp or weft or both are crepe twisted; how tight the twist is and in which direction. It heightens the crepe effect to alternate S and Z twist yarns.

Generally, crepes are lightweight, thin and without a great deal of luster, as luster is obscured by tight twist. *Crepe de chine* is a lustrous crepe, and *chirimen* is a heavy crepe, while *chiffon* is probably the lightest.

Some Silk Crepes

Arabian Crepe. A figured crepe in silk, cotton or worsted. The pattern is made by extra wefts that are cut away at the edge of the figure; the ground is plain crepe.

Canton Crepe. Fine, hard twist Canton silk warp, 14/16 deniers or heavier; thicker, hard twist tram for weft. S and Z twists alternate every two picks, forming a surface of fine cross-ribs. Another version alternates every six picks. Heavier than Crepe de Chine; durable and washes well. Originally exported through Canton.

Chiffon. A very fine crepe woven of fine, 10/12 to 12/14 deniers, tight twist singles both warp and weft. (See also under *Chiffon.*)

Chirimen. A heavy Japanese crepe used for *Furoshiki* (package-wrapping squares). Warp is fine with slight or no twist; weft is very heavy with a crepe twist. The effect is a wavy cross-cording.

Crepe Charmeuse. (See Charmeuse.)

Crepe de Chine. A light, soft and lustrous crepe, heavier than Crepe Georgette, lighter than Canton crepe. Warp is fairly fine, 14/16 deniers, and of almost twist. Hard twist weft is alternated S and Z every two picks, or sometimes pick and pick. The beat is tight, and the result is a surface very finely crinkled, almost smooth, with high luster for a crepe.

Crepe Georgette. Named after Mme. Georgette de la Plante, a designer of Paris. Very fine and sheer, very creped. Both warp and weft are hard twist, and usually both are arranged 2 and 2, or pick and pick, S and Z twists. Tightly woven so the crimps are fine. The construction gives it a good body for its light weight, and it wears well. Although it is not very lustrous, it sparkles in sunlight. Woven raw and piece degummed, it is usually dyed or printed. (See also *Chiffon.*) The yarns of Georgette are two- or three-ply, while those of chiffon are singles.

Fabric Terms

warp — the threads that go lengthwise of a fabric.

weft (woof, filling) — the threads that go crosswise of a fabric, from selvedge to selvedge.

Fabric cut from a bolt is cut across the warp, with the weft, from selvedge to selvedge.

selvedge (selvage) — the edge of a fabric where the weft turns back. Usually has a heavier warp, and sometimes a different weave.

end — a warp thread.

pick (pic) — a single "shot" or "throw" of weft thread, as it goes across the warp once, from selvedge to selvedge.

sett — how closely the warp ends are spaced.

beat — how closely the weft picks are spaced.

e.p.i. — "ends per inch".

p.p.i. — "picks per inch".

S and Z twists:

(hold the yarn vertical)

S twist — twist ascends to the left.

Z twist — twist ascends to the right.

Crepe Meteor. A soft, smooth and lustrous twill-faced crepe. Lightweight, like Crepe Georgette. Soft twist warp, hard twist weft alternating S and Z twist every two picks. Woven raw and piece degummed and dyed. Used for dresses. May be used with the crepe (weft) side as the "face" and the lustrous twill "back" side turned out as trim. Thus sometimes called *Satin Backed Crepe* from the satin-like twill surface.

Flat Crepe. Crepe twist weft crosses a heavy, densely sett warp. Thus the fabric appears smooth, but it has a crepe's stretchiness in the weft direction. Woven raw and piece degummed.

Satin Crepe. Satin weave using crepe yarns. Delicately crimped satin on the face, flat crepe on the back. A very thin, delicate satin used for dresses, suits, linings and traditional Japanese coats. The satin weave may be a relatively short twill satin.

Crepons, Crimps and **Blisters.** That kind of crepe that's woven of different fibered yarns that vary in shrinking properties (see *Crepe*). In Crimps the shrinking process is "printed" to give texture designs. Blisters are figured Crepons woven rather elaborately: the figure is woven as double cloth with the shrinking yarn as one cloth, the unshrinking as the other, while in the ground both yarns are woven together. On shrinking, the top double-cloth Blisters.

Damask (from *Damascus*). Figured cloth where the figure and ground are of contrasting weaves. Usually the figures are in weft satin on a ground of warp satin, all in the same color. The figure is visible because of the different light reflections of the weft-faced and warp-faced weaves. In *Lampas* contrasting colors are used, and sometimes multiple colors, especially in the weft. In *Brocatelle* ground weaves other than satin are used. Nor must the figures be in satin: warp-faced crossed by weft-faced twills are a popular combination.

Five- or eight-shaft satins are usual. These are sometimes called "single" and "double" damasks, respectively. "Double Damask" is also used for a damask where the weft and warp satins are balanced so the fabric is reversible (double faced), or where there are more picks than ends. It is not a precise term.

Exodus 39:3 — ". . . and they did beat the gold into thin plates and cut it into wires, to work it in the blue, and in the purple, and in the scarlet, and in the fine linen, with cunning work."

The colors of the tabernacle — the colors of the Universe: blue for air; scarlet for fire; purple for water, because the purple dye came from the sea; white linen for the earth, from which it grew.

Diapered Fabric. Originally silk from Damascus and Baghdad embroidered all over with small multi-colored designs, arranged to make diamond shapes. Later woven in Europe in white cotton or linen with weave of simple geometric repeats called a diaper weave. *(Wilcox)*

Dupionni, Duppioni, Douppioni, etc. (meaning *doubled*). Doupioni silk is reeled from two cocoons slightly enmeshed because the worms started spinning too close together. It makes a yarn with pronounced but irregular slubs.

Dupionni silk cloth is a plain woven, relatively coarse fabric using dupionni silk for both warp and weft. It is sturdy, substantial, but also soft and flexible. The luster is subdued by the tight plain weave; the texture, which is often compared to linen, takes visual precedence. It is considered very elegant, with the long, irregular slubs in random crossings. Used for dresses, light coats, etc.

Linshang is a Japanese dupionni fabric; *Shantung* is now woven with dupionni as the weft.

Faille. Soft, warp rib silk with small, flat crosswise ribs. A two-ply warp is set close and two or more picks of heavier singles weft are thrown successively in the same shed. This gives the warp-rib effect without using a really heavy, thick weft. The cloth is fine, soft and lustrous, sometimes even glossy. Usually yarn dyed; used for dresses, hats, etc. Faille is a kind of grosgrain, but faille ribs are wider.

Foulard (French: *silk handkerchief*). Thin, light and soft, with a slightly lustrous finish. Usually a 2/2 twill, although sometimes in plain or other weave. More a quality of fabric than a specific weave/yarn combination. Used for handkerchiefs and scarves and for summer dresses. Typically printed in an all-over pattern or dyed plain in the piece.

Fugi Silk. A plain weave fabric of raw, spun silk. May be left raw or be piece degummed. Degummed, it is used for traditional Japanese clothes, underclothes, linings, etc. Fugi silk is of spun silk, *Habutai* of reeled silk; otherwise they look similar, although the hand of the spun Fugi silk is softer. Fugi silk is often a creamy off-white.

Gauze (from *Gaza*, Palestine). In gauze weaves, alternate warps cross around adjacent warps. They are held in this crossed position by the weft. The fabric can be heavy, even very heavy, but "gauze" is usually understood as a light to very light, but firm, open mesh fabric. *Leno* is a gauze mixed with areas of plain or other non-crossing weave. These areas can be used to make patterns in the gauze ground or vice versa. Simple gauzes, like *Boulting cloth*, are used as backing fabric for embroidery and needlepoint. Gauze is also used generally for any light, openly woven fabric, such as *Organza*.

Gossamer. A very soft silk gauze woven plain with one end crossing one end. Used for veils. An example of yarns: 22 deniers warp sett at 44 e.p.i.; 36 deniers weft beat to 80 p.p.i.

Grenadine. A stiff though lightweight gauze which might be either plain or figured. Usually woven with distinct warp stripes. Skein dyed, hard twist organzine is set to give an open texture, then the fabric is heavily glue sized to give a stiff finish. Especially popular in the late 19th century; used for blouses, dresses and neckties. Also woven in worsted and cotton.

Marquisette. A very sheer gauze or leno with open mesh. Lightweight; used for curtains and dresses.

Milanese Cord (after *Milan*, Italy). A warp rib, silk-faced fabric. Cotton cord weft is completely covered by gauze woven silk warp.

Ra. Japanese name for an ancient patterned gauze of Chinese origin. Designs and techniques are similar to what handweavers know as *Tarascan lace:* complex diamond shapes in a very open gauze are spaced on a gauze ground.

Ro. A Japanese leno where rows (picks) of gauze alternate with rows of plain weave, usually in regular order, as three rows plain, three rows gauze. Woven raw and piece de-gummed and dyed. Used for mid-summer kimono, evening dresses, curtains, etc.

Sha. Japanese name for an oriental gauze woven to make small, all-over geometrical lozenge shapes. Typically: three pairs of ends cross, three pairs weave plain; the next pick, those that crossed weave plain and vice versa. Woven raw; used as Ro.

There is an altogether other kind of Sha which is used in Japanese textile printing. It is a very open, very fine, cheese-cloth-like plain gauze. Pasted to heavy stencil paper, it holds open-work stencils in place. It is a truly transparent silk fabric.

"Sha" Gauze

Sha ground is often figured with designs in large circles. To weave the figure, the warp ends are simply not crossed. Then the multi-stranded weft opens out to make an opaque area. This type figured gauze is found in the sleeves of old Chinese Mandarin robes where it is used to exquisite effect.

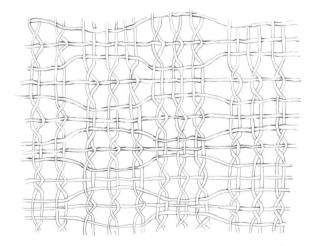

Glacé (see *Shot Silk).*

Gloria. Strong, firmly woven fabric of silk warp and worsted or cotton weft, usually in plain weave. Used for umbrellas and dresses. Gloria of silk and wool was a popular fabric around the turn of the century as it gave a fine, lustrous fabric at relatively low cost. It was piece dyed, either all one color or the silk and wool could be different shades. If the shades are close, this gives a subtle blend color, or if contrasting, a shimmering "shot" effect.

Gold Cloth, Gold Tissue. A modern fabric woven with gold colored metallic warp and silk weft. Used for evening clothes.

Gossamer. A very soft silk *Gauze.*

Grenadine. A stiff, though lightweight, *Gauze.*

Grosgrain (from *gros,* French: *thick).* Plain weave with crossways warp ribs made through using a fine silk warp, closely sett, and a thick weft of silk, cotton or worsted so there are relatively few picks to ends. The result is a firmly woven, closely textured fabric with distinct ribs. The ribbing is finer than in *Faille,* where several wefts are thrown in the same shed, but heavier than in *Poplin.* Woven from skein-dyed yarns, it has a slightly lustrous finish. Considered "formal", it is used for dresses, ribbons, vestments and coats. Durable because of the close weave.

Gros de . . . Applied to many different kinds of cross-ribbed silks constructed similarly to *Grosgrain.*
Gros de Londres. All silk with cross ribs that alternate either fine and coarse or two different colors.
Gros de Tours. Heavy ribbed silk with two or more picks in a shed. Often used as a selvedge weave, as it makes a tight but not bulky fabric.

Habutai, Habutae, Habutaye (said to mean *soft, downy).* A general term applied to silks from Japan which are closely woven but fine and soft. The weave is usually plain, but may be twill or fancy. It is woven raw and piece degummed. Classically, the warp is a loosely-twisted singles and the weft is hand-reeled silk, thus slightly irregular.

Habutai is lustrous, smooth and has a good hand and scrope. It may be light (*China Silk* is sometimes called habutai), medium or heavy weight. Plain woven habutai resembles *Taffeta*, but with a softer hand. Used for clothes, traditional Japanese and modern, and for scarves, neckties and other accessories.

Hakata (from *Hakata* in Kiyushu). A very heavy Japanese warp rib fabric. The weft is much heavier than the warp; the fabric is lustrous, thick and resilient but firm. It is especially used for belts. Woven in many colors for women, and in dark colors for men. It may be sparsely patterned with simple geometric designs formed by supplemental warp floats.

Half Silks. Fabrics woven of silk warp and other fibered weft, or vice versa. For instance, cotton or rayon backed satins. (See also *Bengaline, Gloria, Union Cloth.*)

Honan. *Pongee* from wild silkworms of the Honan area of China. Noted for dyeing well, in distinction to other wild silk pongees.

Illusion. A silk tulle used for veils: ". . . and the Bride wore a veil of Illusion".

Iridescent (see *Shot*).

About Jacquard Designs

The advantage of the drawloom over hand pick-up was automatic, multiple horizontal repeats; vertical freedom could be maintained. The advantages/disadvantages to the Jacquard are automatic vertical repeatability and speed. Classic Jacquard designs tend to be over-blown with much attention to elaborate details, but less to the vision of the design. It seems too easy to become too complicated.

Often Jacquard designs are symmetrical, with one doubled, face-to-face repeat the full width of the cloth. This is an especially difficult format to design for, since there is no inherent rhythm of repeat.

The tragedy of the Jacquard device is not just that it was the first major step in the subjugation of handweaving, of weavers, to machines. But that this device, with its near infinite capacity for design, should have been used so banally. Complexities became an end in themselves. It is difficult to appreciate work such as de LaSalle's because we have been so innundated by cheap and poor imitations.

Jacquard Silks. Patterned fabrics where the pattern is controlled automatically by a mechanical device called a Jacquard after its inventor, Joseph Marie Jacquard (1752-1834). The device, it should be noted, when first introduced, was immediately burned in the streets by the silk weavers of Lyon who (rightly) saw it as a threat to their skill and livelihood.

The Jacquard device makes pattern sheds according to a series of punched cards. It can be part of a power or a hand loom (Jacquard fabrics can be machine or hand woven). It is estimated that at the turn of the century over 5,000 hand weaving Jacquard looms were in operation in Lyon. The Jacquard loom took the place of the ancient draw loom, where the making of the pattern shed was done by a second weaver, usually a boy apprentice called a "draw-boy".

Jacquard devices, substantially the same as the original, are the pattern device for the modern power loom. Any type design or weave can be controlled by them, and the distinctions between "Jacquard", "brocade" and "damask" have become blurred. Even "tapestry" will be used for a pictorial Jacquard, so that all these terms are now used virtually interchangeably.

Japanese Silk (see *China Silk* and *Habutai).*

Jersey Cloth. Silk jersey is a very soft knitted fabric used for sweaters, dresses, underwear and gloves. Piece dyed.

Kinran (Japanese: *gold strip*). A Japanese silk and gold cloth, the silk ground in plain weave with pattern in gold-leafed paper thread.

K'o-ssu. Chinese tapestry weave. All areas are plain weave silk in a weft-faced weave. Yarns are so fine, and the fabric so thin, that it is transparent when held to the light. Similar weave in Japan is known as *Tsuzure-ori,* literally "vine weaving".

Knit. Besides the smooth *Jersey* and the fine *Milanese,* heavier textured spun silk yarns such as bouclés and cords are knit into cloth or clothes. Spun silk yarns are loftier than reeled yarns and are especially nice for hand knits.

Lampas. Multicolored *Damask* or *Brocade*. Very elaborate. Lampas may be woven with double warps and several sets of wefts, reproducing a picture in fine detail by means of a color technique similar to that used in half-tone prints.

Levantine (from *the Levant*). Tight twill-woven silk with a different color on each side. Used for sashes and robes.

Leno (see *Gauze*).

Liberty. Trade name for Liberty of London. Founded in 1875 by Arthur Lasenby Liberty (later Sir Arthur), they are specialists in fine textured silks, cottons and woolens. Originally, and up through at least 1918, these were all dyed with natural dyes, and Liberty colors were noted for their delicacy and permanence (*Thompson*). Much attention is paid to design. William Morris, for instance, designed for Liberty, and many Liberty fabrics are now in museum collections.
Liberty Satin. A standard fabric around the turn of the century: 7-, 8-, 10- or 12-shaft satin woven of raw silk warp and spun silk weft. Piece degummed and dyed; very soft handling.

Macclesfield (see *Spitalfields*).

Marble Silk. Silk with variegated coloring from tie-dyed weft or from printing the warp before weaving. Lightweight, for dresses. (See also *Chiné*.)

Matelassé. A warp-faced, strongly cross-ribbed fabric with pattern. Originally woven as banded double cloth with areas of wadding or heavy threads between the cloths forming a raised pattern. The pattern, usually flowers, showed only as an apparent embossment. Now, figures usually formed by warp floats across the thick ribs.

Milanese. A thin silk or rayon warp-knit fabric used for underwear and gloves.

Milanese Cord (see *Gauze*).

Moiré *(watered).* Cloth with a watered or wavy appearance due to differing light reflections. It is produced on warp or weft ribs by pressing areas of the ribs down flat: the flat areas reflect more light than the ribbed areas. The crushing is done between heated rollers with the fabric damp. Classically, the designs are made by pressing two thicknesses together: where the ribs cross, they are flattened; where one rib comes between the ribs of the other cloth, they remain round. This gives a non-repeating, spontaneous design. Designs can also be engraved on the rollers. With such engraved rollers even taffeta and velvet can be moiréd.

Moiré Antique. The classic moiré, with elongated, irregular patterns.

Moiré à Retours. Moiréd by folding the cloth in half lengthwise and pressing. The design is the same on each half, but reversed ink-blot style.

Moiré Française. A striped moiré done with an engraved roller.

Muslin (from *Mosul* in Iraq). Muslin is a general term for soft, light, open, plain weave fabrics of any fiber. *Mousseline de soie* — silk muslin — is sheer and soft, similar to chiffon, but more openly woven.

Ninon. Basket woven: double warps crossed by double wefts in plain weave. Fine, light and soft, for summer dresses.

Nishiki *(Japanese Brocade).* A figured fabric in multi colors, often with gold or silver threads. Associated with Kyoto, and also woven in other centers in Japan. Directly derived from imported Chinese weaving, old examples of which are preserved in the Shoso-in and the Horyu-ji.

Nishiki means "highly ornamental silk weaving", but the word also connotes "beautiful combinations of colors" rather than any specific weave. Colors are odd in number, usually five or seven, and typically include red, blue, yellow, purple and green, as well as gold metallic. The weave is noted in a prefix as: *aya*-nishiki, *twill* (ground) nishiki.

Ezo-nishiki. Brocade on satin ground; design threads float across the back.

Ito-nishiki. An early kind, woven without gold threads.

Kikko-nishiki. With hexagonal, tortoise-shell pattern, symbolizing longevity.

Tate-nishiki. Warp brocade. The weave is a fine, warp rib faced double cloth. The design is formed through a multicolored warp: each warp place has three warps, each is one of three colors: one color comes to the surface while the other two are at the back. Both surfaces are woven tight and firm. Usually this type nishiki is made with the design in stripes. The stripes are in different color combinations, so that many colors are used in the whole cloth.

Tsuzure-nishiki. Tapestry woven.

Ungen-nishiki. Weft brocade. Weave like the tate-nishiki, only the weft forms the surface. Typically woven as band after band of different designs in rainbows of multi-colored stripes. Freer than tate-nishiki; each stripe can be a different design.

Noil. Woven with yarn spun from the very short silk combings called noils. The noil yarn is typically used in both warp and weft in a balanced plain weave. One unusual kind from India has a very heavy noil weft crossing a thin, thrown warp. The heavy irregular weft gives a slight undulating effect.

Unbleached noil is characterized by flecks of black (chrysalis remains) as well as the tangled balls of fiber formed in carding. The fibers are very short, thus the fabric is subject to wear. As compensation, noil fabrics are relatively thick.

A great attraction of natural silk noil fabric is its muted luster, which gives it a fashionably casual look. It is often called *Raw Silk.*

Organza, Organdy, Organdie. Silk organza is a light, transparent and stiff plain weave. It is woven of singles raw silk and not degummed, as the gum holds the weave in place and gives the characteristic hand. It is dyed without degumming. Used for summer dresses, hats, doll clothes and to line other delicate, sheer fabrics.

Organza is sometimes called "gauze", and a very open, cheesecloth-like gauze used for strengthening paste-resist stencils in Japanese dyeing is sometimes called "organza" (see *Sha* under *Gauze).*

Ottoman (from Ottoman Turks). A heavy warp-faced, ribbed fabric. Warp of silk, heavy weft of silk, worsted or cotton. Also can be all wool. *Ottoman Cord* is woven of thick warps and fine wefts to give ribs running lengthwise.

Paper or **Felt.** A non-woven cloth formed by enmeshing fibers rather than yarns. From the *Encyclopedia Britannica*, Eleventh Edition: "In the modern sense 'paper' may best be described as a more or less thin tissue composed of any fibrous material, whose individual fibres, first separated by mechanical action, are then deposited and felted together. . . ."

We think of paper as thin, and made primarily of cellulose fiber, felt as relatively thick and formed of wool, hair or fur. Their construction is identical although the techniques of forming them vary with the fiber used: cellulose is boiled to separate and swell the fibers then deposited on a screen, drained and compacted. The fibers adhere in the random arrangement and the additional pressure forms and molds them into a tight, strong, homogenous fabric. Felt is formed from fibers whose surface is scaly, thus, in felt, the fibers actually interlock through the little barbs on the surface scales. Felt is made by arranging the fibers in a random fashion, then rubbing them together so that the scales are raised and the fibers interlock.

Silk is neither cellulose nor scaly. But by using the paper-forming techniques, a lustrous, soft felt can be produced. The fibers are first chopped into ½" lengths, then boiled in pure water, spread out onto a screen, drained and pressed. This very simple process makes a beautiful cloth, but it is not very strong. Strength and flexibility can be increased by adding animal glue size, or by admixing a smaller or greater proportion of cellulose or wool fiber.

Japanese papers (which are made from many different plants' fibers) may have strands of silk incorporated for decoration. Especially elegant are glossy white silk thrums meandering through natural light brown colored bark paper.

Peau de Cygne (French: *swan's skin*). Tightly woven silk satin with a soft, lustrous finish. Strong, closely woven in the gum and piece dyed. A slight pebbled effect is gotten as the wefts stitch down two adjacent warps at a time.

Peau de Soie (French: *silk skin*). A thin, very soft silk satin distinguished by a dull luster and slightly grainy or cross-ribbed surface. The face is a five-shaft warp satin, and the best grades are backed with an additional 15-thread weft satin, so the cloth is reversible. Used for dresses.

Pekin, Pekin Stripe. Striped silk fabrics where the stripes are of different weaves. Usually satin and grosgrain alternating, but also plain, rib, gauze, velvet, etc.

Plush (see also *Velvet*). Plush has a longer pile than velvet, over ⅛" long. The pile may be of worsted, mohair or silk; spun wild silk is used for sealskin plush.

Pongee (said to mean "home-made"). A wild silk fabric. Originally pongee was handwoven from hand-reeled Chinese tussah silk. Woven raw and piece degummed, old pongee is soft and supple with a pronounced but refined luster and natural honey beige color.

Wildly popular in the '20s, many different kinds of imitations were woven, and the character of pongee has changed considerably. Contemporary pongee is a relatively stiff, tightly and durably woven medium to heavy weight fabric. Yarns are usually reeled wild silk, but white silk may be used, especially for warp. *Fugi pongee* means spun silk yarns are used; other names, such as *Honan pongee*, denote the area in China from which the fabric originated. Natural colors range from off-white (sometimes said to be bleached) to dark honey beige.

Poplin. Originally a finely corded, lightweight silk fabric, now woven in other fibers.

Raw Silk. Woven of undegummed, thus raw, silk. It may be very thin and open, as organza, or coarse and heavy, or anything in between. Usually woven of reeled silk, as spun silk is degummed before spinning, but it can be woven of partially degummed spun silk. Much raw silk fabric is in fact partially degummed — otherwise it would be very stiff. Raw silk has less of the luster and sparkle associated with degummed silk, but it becomes softer and more lustrous as it is worn. The gum gives strength and durability. Unbleached noil fabric is also called raw silk.

Rep, Repp (from *rib*). A pronounced cord or rib effect. Ribs are made when one set of yarns is heavier and stiffer than the other. The fine yarns bend around the heavy one which form the cords. Rep cords are often completely covered by the finer yarn. In a *warp rep* fabric the warp is fine and the weft is the heavier yarn; the ribs go across the fabric (selvedge to selvedge) and are called *cross ribs*. In a *weft rib* fabric the warps are heavy and form lengthwise ribs covered by the fine weft. The simplest reps are plain weave, but more complex rep and *cannele* weaves can accentuate the ribbed effect (see *Oelsner, Watson* and *Wolfensberger*). Some ribbed silks are Bengaline, Faille, Gros de Tours, Grosgrain, Hakata, Matelassé, Ottoman and Poplin.

Samite, Samit. Twill-faced patterned silk: the weave used in ancient Persian and Byzantine figured silks. Constructed as ungen-nishiki (see *Nishiki*).

Sari Silk, Saree Silk, Indian Silk. Very thin and gossamer plain weave silks handwoven in India for saris. They have marvelous natural luster and whiteness. Best qualities probably are close to the original handwoven "China silk". Sari silk is so light that a yard of it, 45" wide, may weigh less than an ounce. The creamy hand of the better quality sari silks is unique and indescribably sensuous. The whiteness, luster and light weight make it ideal for dyeing, but it is not closely woven, so must be handled with care. The better the quality, the denser the weave and the creamier the hand. Handwoven sari silks show the dense-to-thinned-out beating of the weft in fairly regular spacings of about 4" that are characteristic of this type of fly shuttle handweaving. Technically a weaving fault, these irregularities add a nice character to the fabric. Dyed or printed in five- or six-yard lengths for use as saris.

Indian tussahs are also handwoven in 45" widths. They have good luster and sparkle, and good dyeability, but they may be very loosely woven.

Figured Sari Silks. Brocaded designs are concentrated at one edge, and sometimes at the ends, of five- to six-yard lengths of 45" wide sari silk. The placement of the design shows best when the material is draped into a sari. The pattern thread is often metallic; formerly, very fine pure gold wires were used.

Satin (said to derive fron *Zaytung*, the Chinese name for the fabric. Satin is a weave especially identified with silk. It is

SATINS

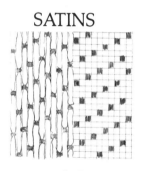

7-shaft
"Satin Merveilleux"

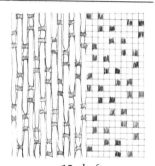

12-shaft
double-stitched,
warp-ways
"Satin Grec"

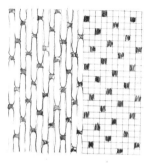

8-shaft
"Satin Duchesse"

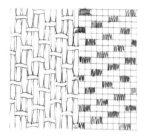

8-shaft
double-stitched,
weft ways
"Peau de Soie"

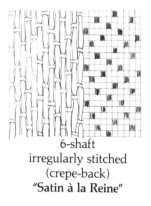

6-shaft
irregularly stitched
(crepe-back)
"Satin à la Reine"

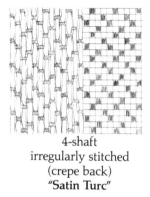

4-shaft
irregularly stitched
(crepe back)
"Satin Turc"

Another 4-shaft satin:
thread 1, 2, 3, 4;
treadle 1,3,1; 2,4,2; 3,1,3; 4,2,4

par excellence the weave to show off silk's luster and experience its richness. Have you ever held a skein of yarn and wished its lush visual texture and hand could be transferred directly into fabric? Satin is the weave that does this. In satin, the warp threads literally float over long areas of the surface of the cloth. The floating warps are stitched down to make a firmly woven cloth that still preserves the visual qualities of the freely draping yarn. The different patterns made by the stitching-down weft threads give rise to the many different types of satins. Satin is smooth, soft and lustrous, but because the weave consists of long surface floats, it is weak to friction and surface wear.

Satin Back, Satin Backed. A fabric whose reverse is satin; the face may be any weave but is usually a crepe or a twill. Used, for instance, for a blouse where decorative rolled seams show the satin back. Very pleasant to wear as the soft satin surface is next to the skin.

Satin Crepe. A satin woven with crepe-twist (very tightly twisted) weft so that it is elastic in the weft direction.

Satin, Crepe Back. Satin with the weave tie-downs arranged in a random manner, as in a crepe weave. The back looks like crepe while the face is satin.

Satin de Lyon. A fine quality historical satin, formerly woven at Lyon, France, center of European silk weaving. All silk, yarn dyed and very lustrous. The name was later used for a cheaper imitation.

Satin, Double Faced. Heavy, reversible satin woven with two warps, one for the front satin and one for the back. Peau de Soie may be woven as a double-faced satin, with the reverse an extra weft satin.

Satin Duchesse. Very rich, heavy and lustrous all-silk satin woven with seven to 12 harnesses. May have a spun silk weft. Originally woven in black only, with no pattern, for dresses.

Satin Façonné. Has a Jacquard pattern on a satin ground.

Satin, Half-Silk. Silk satins are often backed with other fibers: cotton, wool and now commonly rayon. These do not affect its appearance, as the weft hardly shows on the surface, but they do affect the feel and hand.

Satin Merveilleux ("marvelous"). Soft, fine, almost imperceptibly twilled satin with a glossy finish. Used for dresses.

Satin, Messaline. Named for Messalina, wife of Emperor Claudius. A five-harness satin, very soft, drapy and lightweight, but closely woven, and finished to a high luster on both sides, so reversible. Skein dyed; used for dresses.

Satin Régence. A very costly dress fabric of the early part of this century. Described as "a rich satin surface with fine sunken lines extending across from selvage to selvage".

Satin Rhadame. A twilled satin with fine twill lines running diagonally across the surface. Sometimes cotton backed.

Satin Royal. Very fine and costly all-silk double-faced twilled satin, used for dresses.

Satin Surah. Medium-heavy weight dress fabric with a twilled surface and lustrous satin finish. Very soft.

Satin Taffeta. Satin face and taffeta (plain weave) back.

Satin, Twill. The stitch-downs are arranged diagonally, in a twill. (See *Twill, Charmeuse, Damask, Liberty Satin, Peau de Cygne, Peau de Soie.*)

Schappe Silk. Fabric woven of spun silk yarns. In Europe this refers specifically to schapped (fermentation degummed) spun silk.

Serge. Tightly woven twill cloth. Ancient Persian figured silks often had a tight twill serge as their face weave.

Shantung. Named for the province of Shantung, China, the source of the original type cloth: a plain woven, relatively rough fabric of hand reeled, tussah wild silk. It was heavier than pongee, and irregular due to slubs and occasional imperfections in the yarn. Now woven of white silk, typically with doupionni silk as the weft, for its slubbed effect. The heavy weft and fine warp give a slight cross ribbing. Shantung can be very white and very lustrous, according to the quality of the weft. It is a highly distinctive fabric: the knubbly, corded texture and substantial feel, combined with the high luster and whiteness, give it a quiet and refined, yet robust character.

Shot Silks (also called *Glacé, Irridescent* and *Changeable Silks).* An irridescent color effect achieved by using contrasting colors in warp and weft, usually in a balanced plain weave fabric (taffeta). Gives a shimmering effect, especially where there are soft folds: the cloth appears first one color, then the other as the angle of view changes. (See also *Chameleon Taffeta).*

Spitalfields and **Macclesfield.** Major English silk weaving centers renowned for very fine count silk weaving. In one typical example small stylized leaves float over a satin ground sett at 280 warps to the inch. These areas were settled by Protestants fleeing religious persecution on the Continent during the 16th and 17th centuries. Spitalfields, a district of London, no longer is engaged in silk weaving. Macclesfield, in the north, continues as a textile and silk weaving center.

Spun Silk. Fabric woven of spun silk yarns. Often the warp is reeled silk, the weft spun silk. Spun silk fabrics tend to be thicker, but have a softer hand than reeled silk fabrics. They may wear more quickly than comparable fabrics of reeled silk because the fibers are shorter and often derived from the weaker parts of the cocoon. (See also *Noil, Schappe,* and *Fugi* silks and *Tsumugi).*

Surah. Named for *Surat,* India, source of the original fabric. A light, soft, twill silk woven with fine organzine warp and fine tram weft. Skein-dyed and reversible. (See also *Satin Surah.)*

Taffeta (from *Taftah,* Persian: *to spin).* Plain weave silk, thin, closely woven and glossy. The weave may be balanced plain or with thicker weft to give a slight cross-ribbing. The close texture gives a resilient hand to the fabric, a delicate crispness. Woven of degummed and skein-dyed yarn, at one time it was heavily weighted.

Taffeta originated in Persia and was woven in Europe in the early Middle Ages — one of the first Western-woven silk fabrics. Formerly, hard-twist yarns were used so it was rather stiff and heavy. Now it is usually woven lighter with softer-twist yarns. Used especially for dresses, blouses and linings.

Taffeta is also used synonymously with "plain weave silk fabric", especially when describing ground fabrics for brocades and velvets.

Chameleon Taffeta. A three-color shot effect: plain weave in three contrasting colors, one in the warp and two in the weft, going pick-and-pick into the same shed.

Chiffon Taffeta. Good quality taffeta treated with heat and pressure to make it very soft and lustrous.

Glacé Taffeta. Woven of contrastingly colored warp and weft. (See *Shot* silk.)

Paper Taffeta. Lightweight; given a special finish to make it very crisp, like paper.

Tissue Taffeta. Very lightweight and transparent.

Pigment Taffeta. Especially dyed yarns are used, so the fabric has a dull surface.

Taffetine. Plain weave with organzine warp and heavier silk or cotton weft. Light, stiff and tight woven, like taffeta. Used for linings.

Thai Silk. Medium to very heavy handwoven silks from Thailand. Plain weave, usually balanced, closely woven and very lustrous.

Tsumugi. A Japanese fabric handwoven of handspun silk in both warp and weft. Originally woven by farmers to make use of waste cocoons. It may be plain white, or dyed in "splashed" patterns *(Kasuri)*, or be woven in stripes. Made in many different weights, medium to very heavy, and in the narrow widths that are used for Kimono. The handspun yarn is heavily sized before weaving to make it easy to handle, and after weaving only some of the matte sizing is steamed off. The fabric then wears soft and lustrous with extra body and durability from the size.

Tsumugi now often has a reeled silk warp. *Yuk-tsumugi* is used to denote all-handspun tsumugi. It is a time-honored national fabric of Japan, highly valued as both simple and rustic, yet possessing a unique elegance of luster and calmness of mood.

Tulle. Named for *Toul,* France. A plain silk netting, very fine and with a very small mesh. Tulle is now usually made of nylon — the ubiquitous nylon net. Silk tulle is very delicate and sheer, although it is often heavily sized. Netted from 9/11 to 12/14 deniers, finest quality silk yarn. Used for ballet dresses, veils and trims.

Tussah, Tussur, Tussore, etc. Named after the wild silk of which it is woven. A plain weave fabric in the natural light beige, honey tan or fawn of tussah silk. The fabric may be of reeled or spun yarns, or a combination. (Chinese tussah silk is often reeled.) At one time tussah silk fabric was imitated in cotton and exported to the Orient! (See also *Pongee.*)

Twill. Twill is a weave in which warp threads cross more than one weft at a time, and vice versa. The crossings are staggered in such a way that they form diagonal lines. In the simplest twill, each warp goes over two then under two wefts. The next warp does the same, but is staggered by one weft/warp. The twill weave makes a fabric that is denser but more supple than a comparable plain weave fabric. Silk twills can be thin and delicate (Surah) or thick and heavy (Serge). (See also *Bombazine, Cachemire de Soie, Crepe Meteor, Foulard, Levantine, Samite* and *Satin Twill.*)

TWILLS

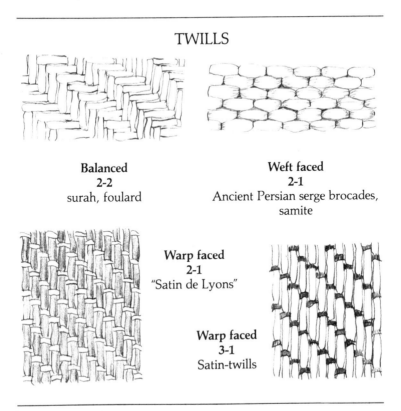

Balanced
2-2
surah, foulard

Weft faced
2-1
Ancient Persian serge brocades,
samite

Warp faced
2-1
"Satin de Lyons"

Warp faced
3-1
Satin-twills

Umbrella Silk. All-silk taffeta, twill, or Gloria or Union Cloth with silk warp and cotton weft, tightly woven to shed water. Often woven striped or with fancy borders.

Union Cloth. A combination (union) of fibers, for instance, silk warp and cotton weft.

Velour (French: *velvet*). At one time a silk and wool velvet with long coarse pile. Now used for a knitted pile fabric, or loosely for velvet or plush.

Velvet (from *velluto*, Italian: *shaggy*). A warp pile fabric, velvet has a short, soft, dense pile. Silk velvet is glossy, soft and lightweight. It is often of spun silk and sometimes the backing fabric is cotton. For the pile, tussah silk is especially used because of its extra strength and resiliency. Long pile of lustrous, natural fawn tussah can imitate sealskin and furs. Cut velvet pile deepens and intensifies colors.

Behring Seal. A coat and suit velvet or plush with natural fawn colored tussah pile in imitation of sealskin. Sometimes the tips of the pile are dyed for extra effect.

Chiffon Velvet. A very light, soft and pliable velvet: "a width could be drawn through a wedding ring." The pile is brushed down while damp. It is not so flat as mirror or panné velvet, and has a shaded luster.

Double-faced Velvet, Chenille. The weft is a chenille yarn that gives the effect of velvet on both sides.

Mirror Velvet. The pile is pressed down flat in different directions.

Nacré. Changeable colored with back of one color and pile of another.

Panné Velvet. A lightweight velvet with a long pile that is pressed down flat for a unique luster.

Plush. Plush has longer pile than velvet — over ⅛".

Uncut Velvet. The looped pile is left uncut. Designs can be made by cutting some areas of the pile and leaving other areas uncut. The cut pile reflects less light and appears darker than the uncut loops.

Utrecht Velvet. Silk or mohair pile velvet used for upholstery.

Voile (French: *veil*). A sheer, very open plain weave fabric of silk or other fiber. Fine spun silk yarns for both warp and weft are given a hard twist and are gassed for extra smoothness. The hand is crisp.

"The cutter, who works at an ordinary wooden bench, has no tool except a small sharp chisel with a V-shaped point . . .

"The cutting artist lays the piece of unfinished velvet on his bench, and proceeds to carve into the pattern with his chisel, just as though he were shading the lines of the design with a steel pencil. When the pattern is lightly traced, he uses his knife delicately; when the lines are strong and the shadows heavy, he makes the point pierce deeply. In short the little chisel becomes in his fingers a painter's brush . . .

"The veining of a cherry petal, for example, the tessellation of a carp's scales, the serration of a leaf's edge — all these lines remain intact, spared by the cutter's tool, while the leaf itself, or the petal, or the scales of the fish, have the threads forming them cut so as to show the velvet nap and to appear in soft, low relief."

Encyclopedia Britannica, Eleventh Edition

Chapter 8
CARE & HANDLING

ine silks need careful handling simply because they are so fine. Heavier silks, especially wild silks, can be handled like a fine staple wool.

Care of silk is similar to care of wool. In our age of machine washable everything it's important to keep firmly in mind that silk must be handled with care and respect. Silk's luster is the quality most sensitive to damage. Careless handling may destroy the luster and eventually damage the durability of the fiber.

All natural silk is washable, except for some fabric with embossed or moiré designs. That is, all silk can be washed in mild soap and lukewarm water using the proper care according to its form: very fine yarns need care not to tangle; spider's web gossamer fabric needs care not to displace threads; laces and antique silks need care not to be torn in handling; soft spun and short fibered yarns and their fabrics need care not to felt.

Soaps, Alkali and Silk

Soap is made by combining fats with strong alkalis like lye (sodium hydroxide) or potash (potassium hydroxide). The result has an affinity for dirt, and the excess alkali usually present attracts grease.

Protein fibers, silk, wool, hair, skin and leather are harmed by this excess alkali. For one thing, they need to retain their natural oils, fats and waxes to remain pliant. Silk does not start out with a great deal of natural fat so it is important none is lost. Some dye processes even end with oiling the silk.

Secondly, alkali, especially hot alkali, attacks protein, eventually disintegrating it. Silk is especially vulnerable because the fiber is so fine. Damage appears first as a diminution of luster.

Neutral soaps such as *Ivory* have had the excess alkali washed out. Other soaps like *Woolite* have been especially treated so they dissolve in cold water. Detergents are a kind of synthetic soap derived from petroleum. They are not inherently alkaline, but alkali is added to most detergents to make them more effective. *Joy* and *Ivory Liquid* are non-alkaline detergents that may be used on silk.

Because of the harmful effects of excess alkali, it's best not only to use a neutral, non-alkaline soap, but also to use a soft, non-alkaline water, and to neutralize any possible traces of alkali with a little acid towards the end of rinsing.

If your water is hard and scums in rinsing, or refuses to suds with the mild soap, start saving rain water as a source of pure, soft water. (In some areas rainwater may be polluted; try distilled water.) Meanwhile add a little washing soda (sodium carbonate) to the soap; add only just enough to get it to suds. Then add pure white vinegar to the rinse waters — enough to dissolve the scum. Try to give a final rinse in pure, soft water.

There are some finishes — surface coatings and sizings — that would need to be redone after washing. These may be found in old silks. And one would not water wash a fabric whose colors proved not fast. But silk, the fiber, is emphatically washable.

Some silk fabrics can even be machine washed: on the delicate or wool cycle and enclosed in a case. The delicate or wool cycle uses cool or warm water and has a short agitation.

An enclosing case is important. It protects the silk from being pulled out of shape. A pillow case works well, with the open end basted or tied; a nylon stocking is good for small pieces like scarves.

Many silk fabrics can be machine dried: on delicate setting and enclosed in a case or dried individually. The delicate setting uses hardly any heat so there is no danger of overheating the silk. A loose case will keep pieces fron tangling, or dry one at a time. The tumble-blow drying leaves fabrics soft and fluffy. Many times ironing isn't needed afterwards, so it can be a real advantage in care. As with any fiber, don't allow silk to overdry.

Yarn, spinning fiber and any delicate or older silk, especially if it shows signs of wear, *must be washed by hand.* With hand washing, care can be more specific than in a washing machine.

It's difficult to give fast rules for each textile has its own qualities, and each craftsperson an individual style. I always hand wash silk because of the closer observation and greater control. Experience is the only sure guide to which sturdier fabrics can be, or even prefer being, machine washed. However, delicate and old fabrics should always be carefully hand-washed, and in many cases this should be done on a supporting screen as suggested below.

Handwashing silk is not such a terrible chore! Silk is so light that washing goes very quickly. We get to experience the material in another form: wet silk is very sensuous. Besides, with all the effort given to dyeing, weaving, sewing, etc., the few minutes it takes to wash it when needed is, after all, miniscule care.

As with any fiber, silk that is worn next to the skin should be washed frequently. The salts and acids of perspiration should not be left on fibers for a long time, just as we do not like to leave them on our own skin.

To Handwash Silk

Lukewarm — wrist warm — water is preferred over cold. Silk, like skin, prefers the water neither too hot nor too cold. If you treat your silk as if it were your skin, you will never damage it. All temperature changes should be gradual.

Soap must be chosen with care. Ivory soap, either Flakes or Snow, is the best. It is a "mild" or "neutral" soap in distinction to "strong" or "alkaline" soaps or detergents. Ivory must be dissolved in a little hot water first, then cold is added to make the lukewarm bath. Before adding cold, be sure the soap is completely dissolved — swish it around until it's nice and sudsy.

Squeeze suds gently through sturdy material. For delicate stuffs see handling suggestions below. For extra dirty areas on tightly woven fabrics, lay the area over one palm and squeeze-pat concentrated suds through it with fingers of the other hand full of soap from a bar of Ivory. This method can remove even grease and soot, but the fabric must be sturdy for the process is liable to displace threads.

Do not wring silk fabric. Squeeze it gently or, better, just let it drip.

Even so-called neutral soap is slightly alkaline. A little acid in the next to last rinse will neutralize any trace of alkali left from the washing. Pure white vinegar is perfect to use for the acid. Add about one tablespoon per quart of water to the next to last rinse. A stronger acid can be used here to give the pronounced scrunchiness known as scrope.

There is one kind of patterned silk that is usually not washable: the embossed-design or moiré silk. The silk fibers swell in water and obliterate the pressed-in design.

Be sure any color is fast before you begin to wash.

Handwashing Delicate Silks

A support of some kind is always a help in preventing loosely woven silks from "pulling". They're especially likely to pull at seams, a reason that delicate silks are best used for unseamed stuffs like scarves and saris. Knits, also, should be washed using some kind of support. A support can be a mesh basket, a collander, a thin cloth held at the corners or sewn into a bag, or, for small pieces, a nylon stocking knotted at the open end.

Anything very delicate, as lace or old silk possibly damaged by over-weighting, should be washed on a full-support screen. In severe cases a double screen is needed, with the

Cleaning of Old Silks

If you have an old and valuable silk which needs cleaning, it is worth searching out a cleaner that has experience in handling old textiles. Ask the curator of textiles at the nearest museum or University where they send their silks to be cleaned.

If there is no adequate service near you, several conservators and cleaners specializing in old textiles will accept pieces by mail. Procedures and fees vary, so contact in advance:

Virginia Cleaners
2109 Virginia Street
Berkeley, CA 94709

Museum of American Textile History
Textile Conservation Center
800 Massachusetts Ave.
North Andover, MA 01845

---

fabric totally encased. A screen can be made from cheesecloth tacked to a painter's canvas stretcher. Nylon window screening is also good and more durable. Lay the frame on a table top outside or over a sink or bathtub inside. Always work in the shade, out of direct sunlight.

Gently pour or spray on a soap solution and work it in with the fingers/palm by gently pat-pressing it down. If it is on a table, the frame will hold the solution in. Tilt it slightly to drain. Rinse the fabric several times in the same way it was washed. Don't forget the slightly acid rinse. Dry in place.

If the fabric is very heavy there is no need for a screen as the fabric will swell and soak up enough soapy water for washing needs. Work on a slightly tilted table or board. A fine-holed hose sprinkler can sometimes be used for rinsing: lay cheesecloth over the top of the fabric if necessary to blunt the force of the spray.

Whatever structure is used, the important principle is to wash and dry flat-out and in place. Any handling of delicate silk while wet can be disastrous, as silk's increase in weight from water can be phenomenal: one-half pound of silk can weigh as much as five pounds in a dripping wet state. Also, in the case of felty fiber, it's the water passing through that disturbs the fibers and "felts" them.

Washing Handwovens

In handwovens, there may be a problem with the felting of yarn floats if the yarn is short fibered or loosely twisted. Handle as a delicate fabric and wash by irrigation only, no squeeze-patting. Work with the screen on a table or board. Tilt the table and introduce soapy and rinse waters at one edge of the frame. Let them flow through at a slow pace, so as not to disturb fibers. Dry in place. Fluff when almost dry.

On the other hand, to emphasize the fluffiness possible with this combination of yarn and weave, one might want to machine wash the pieces, enclosed in cases in the recommended way. Then machine dry them, outside of the cases. This gives a light and lofty fabric and is especially good for making soft and fluffy fringes. *(Sara Lee Futterman)*

Drying

Silk fabric can be let drip dry. Most silk is so fine that it drys very quickly. If the fabric is heavy, it can be rolled in a towel or spun in a washing machine (line the basket or put the silk in a case) to take out excess water.

Dry silk in the shade or inside, not in direct sun. Overheating while dry may damage the silk, and some colors are very sensitive to sunlight when wet. Logwood purple, for instance, will redden if dried in strong direct sunlight. If your line is in the sun, cover the silk with a thin white cloth.

Don't just leave the silk until it's dry! The damp and the almost-dry states are the perfect times for untangling, defelting and straightening yarn, for smoothing wrinkles and straightening edges of fabrics, and for fluffing up spinning fiber preparatory to spinning. And silk may dry stiff if it's not handled a bit while it's drying. Fluff it up or shake it a little two or three times while the silk goes from damp to dry.

Ironing

Silk needs to be ironed — unless a crinkly effect is part of the design or the piece is a soft handwoven that needs only a little fluffing up while drying.

As with hand washing, hand ironing is out of practice just now. But it's not difficult work. It's fun to watch the iron smooth out the crinkles and dramatically change the form of the fabric so quickly and easily.

Electric irons are conveniently marked with a "silk" setting, which is usually a range. (It's between rayon and wool in case it's not marked.) Fine silks will take the lower end of the range, heavy silks and tussahs need the high end. Use the low end, too, if you're working slowly, say on pleats or fine details. For flat pieces an ironing board isn't necessary: a few layers of sheeting on a table work as well.

General suggestions include ironing edges and seams first, then the flat surfaces, stroking with the grain. That is, with the warp or weft rather than on the bias.

See if it's okay to iron directly — if no "shine" develops. Then use a dry iron if the fabric is thin. Steam is helpful on heavy silks, but steam seems to cause most thin fabrics to pucker. If a too smooth and metallic looking shine does develop, either iron on the wrong side of the fabric or use a piece of plain white cloth — a press cloth — between fabric and iron.

Special Cases. If a fine silk is stubbornly wrinkled, for instance, if it's been tie-dyed, this procedure works well: first iron it with the dry iron; then press-iron it using a damp press cloth; then iron it dry again until all wrinkles are out and the fabric is dry.

Handwoven fabric rarely needs more than a very light pressing. Yarns are usually substantial and resilient so the fabric doesn't wrinkle much in the first place. Then, texture is very important and a heavy ironing would smash it all flat. Often it is enough to smooth it out by hand while it's slightly damp and let it dry flat. Where the fabric allows, tumble drying (delicate setting) also obviates the need to iron.

To iron out wrinkles yet preserve the texture of the yarns and weave, lay the fabric to be ironed on another fabric with a similar texture depth. For instance, a heavy flannel for a plain weave, relatively smooth texture; terry toweling for a pattern weave texture — sheared terry is better than looped, and velvet is also good. For really deep textures use several layers of towels, and the one just under the top layer can be damp for extra effect. Use a similarly soft-textured fabric as a press cloth

Velvets & Moirés

Velvet is generally not ironed: it is steamed. The easiest way to do this at home is to hang the velvet in the bathroom while you take a hot shower.

Pressed-flat areas in lofty fabrics, such as velvet or cords, can be used for design. Panné or crushed velvet is an example where designs may be printed by ironing areas flat. Heavy silks with pronounced ribs may be embossed or moiréd. Embossing is done using raised or etched rollers, with heat, pressure, and sometimes steam to set the design.

Embossed or moiréd designs, and crushed or panné velvets cannot be water washed or steamed. The water causes the fibers to swell, thus obliterating the design. Such fabrics must be dry cleaned.

---

on top and "press" by gently holding the iron just at the level of the fabric without actually pressing it down. If the press cloth is damp and the iron held in place a few seconds, the result will be to steam the material under it. This usually works better than a "steam" iron. And it avoids putting the silk in direct contact with hot metal that can produce an artificial, too-smooth and metallic looking "shine".

Embroidery, especially if it uses cord-silk, does not want to be pressed flat. To finish, iron it face down over velvet or several layers of flannel. Because of the different temperatures needed to finish linen, cotton, wool and silk, it is wiser to embroider silk onto silk or wool rather than onto linen or cotton unless the piece is purely decorative and will not need ironing.

Half Silks. Silk woven with another fiber as either warp or, usually, weft, is called half-silk. It can be rather difficult to iron well because of the different temperatures needed for the two types of fibers. Use the lower temperature of the two. Rayon-backed satin irons out fairly well by using the rayon setting (slightly cooler than silk) and ironing on the rayon side. If necessary, finish with a quick touch-up on the silk side at the lowest silk setting. Wool-silk blends iron well at the silk setting (slightly cooler than wool). Cotton-backed satin, once common, has been replaced by rayon-backed. Cotton-backed satin must have been very difficult to iron, as the temperature needed for cotton is a lot higher than allowable for silk.

Handweavers often blend yarns/fibers. Because the yarns are heavy and resilient, they don't need a lot of ironing and the disparity of temperatures isn't so important. Always use the lowest setting (that is, the highest allowable temperature for the most sensitive fiber). This can be very low for synthetics that melt easily — a good reason to be sure that "silk" is silk. Use a damp press cloth in stubborn cases. Always drip dry such blends if they cannot be tumbled dried (delicate setting). As soon as they no longer drip, lay flat to finish drying and fluff as much as possible in the near dry state. Then ironing may not be needed.

Shrinkage

Silk shrinks when it gets wet because water swells the fibers. They find a new position and are set there when they dry. They can be repositioned by stretching and pressing so the yarn/fabric assumes its original shape.

To be very effective it helps to have some equipment: stretcher frames for fabric and a lustering hook for yarn. Fabric can be stretched while slightly damp, held in place and ironed dry. Yarn can be put on a hook, then stretched by simultaneously pulling and twisting. Or it can be reskeined while slightly damp and let dry in position.

These processes pull out the fibers, and by placing them more parallel, increase their luster. But this is at the expense of elasticity. "Shrunk" yarns have more elasticity than ones which have been stretched. In many cases it's worth trading a little luster for more elasticity as this means easier care and more comfortable wear.

Crepes and handwoven fabrics are the most shrink-prone and shrinkage has to be taken into account in weaving. The amount of shrinkage may vary from 0% to 15% or more, depending on the yarns used, their sett and the weave. I use 5% as an average for tight weaves and plied yarns, 10% for loose weaves and singles yarns. Warp-ways shrinkage is usually a little more than weft-ways because of the tension on the warp during weaving.

Pre-shrinking. Always pre-shrink silk fabric before cutting it to sew. A thorough wetting out in lukewarm water is all that's needed. If you dye or wash the fabric, that functions as a pre-shrinking.

You can also pre-shrink yarn for handweaving/knitting. This will cut later shrinkage considerably. Hand-dyed or boiled-off yarns will have already shrunk their maximum in the dyeing process. (However, this wouldn't usually be true of commercially dyed silks as they would have been stretched out again.) So, in combining natural with hand-dyed silk, the natural should also be pre-shrunk. If it is not, the natural yarns will shrink after weaving but the dyed won't. This will form puckers and drawn-in areas that need vigorous blocking to re-square. On the other hand, this difference in shrinkages could be used for seersucker or crepe effects.

To pre-shrink silk yarns, or to shrink silk fabrics, simply wet out thoroughly. The most thorough wetting out is had by immersing the silk in pure water and heating it to a near boil. Let the silk set overnight in the cooling water.

Another way to shrink yarns and fabrics is to steam them with a steam iron. Lay the silk out on the board, set the iron to "cotton", and, with the steam on, hold the iron *above* the yarn or fabric — do not let it touch — and watch the silk shrink up. It is finished when it stops shrinking. Turn the skeins or cloth so every part is done. (Suggested by Jan Burnam, Mendocino.) This method has the advantage that it doesn't felt yarns or leave fabrics in need of a subsequent ironing.

Dyed Silks

It is very important to be sure dyed silk is color-fast to water washing *before* you wash it. Spot test the color in an inconspicuous place: put a few drops of soapy water on the color, let set a minute, then blot with a white cloth. If the white cloth shows color, or if the soapy spot has changed color, it won't take washing too well. According to dry cleaners, all colors except oil based paint colors are fast to dry cleaning.

If it must be water washed, wet out in clear water, then wash as quickly as possible. Blot dry immediately between layers of white cotton. Should the problem be bleeding of

Finishing Handwovens

There is no general rule for the finishing of handwoven silks. There are too many variables: yarns used, the weave, and the vision in mind for the final result. Too, every weaver has an individual style and manner of working. Techniques comfortable and easy for one may be clumsy and inefficient for another. Try out many different ways, then choose; or follow the method which seems most natural to you.

Silk, as it comes from the loom, may be very stiff. How stiff depends on the yarns used and the weave's tightness. I know of one fine silk, a simple textured weave using sewing thread for both warp and weft. When I saw it, it was soft as a handkerchief, but when it came from the loom it was like car seat vinyl.

A period of breaking-in needs to be allowed for. Just wearing or using the silk will soften it, but to speed this process some weavers wash their fabrics (and fluff while drying); others have found a simple ironing removes the stiffness.

I like to let my fabrics wear in. Besides, this gives me a great excuse to wear them awhile before passing them on — and I get to better know my own work.

Other weavers always wash the piece after it comes from the loom. This helps remove reed marks, takes care of all shrinkage, and, by swelling the yarns in water, returns the loft that may have been pressed out while the yarns were wound on the warp beam and bobbins.

If the warp has been sized, the sizing must be washed out, unless its added stiffness is an asset.

The washing machine is a tool and like any tool should be tested before being wholeheartedly embraced. Don't throw all and any silk into a washing machine! Always consider carefully . . . or better, do a test wash on a piece of the fabric before consigning a whole creation.

If you choose to wash by machine, try skipping the spin-dry cycle. It tends to crumple fine silks and crush in wrinkles. With heavy, lofty fabrics it may flatten texture.

Where washing is not needed, a light ironing is often enough to soften the stiffness that newly woven silks tend to. A steam iron, held above but not touching the cloth, is very good for shrinking the cloth without disturbing its surface. Or a light ironing with a dry press-cloth may be enough to give that finished look. For other pieces, a heavy pressing with a damp cloth may give the effect wanted.

Brushing is a technique that can soften both the hand and the surface texture of a bourette piece. Use a natural, firm-bristled brush. Steam the silk under a press cloth and, while it is still warm and damp, brush lightly across the warp and/or across the weft, as appropriate to the piece. *(Barbara Nordin.)*

Silks that have been pressed too flat can be plumped by steaming: hang them in the bathroom while you take a hot shower. This technique can also restore elasticity to too-stretched yarns.

Finally, some weavers prefer to leave their work with a professional cleaner for finishing.

colors, immediately iron the fabric completely dry between layers of white cotton. A final rinse in an acid solution may also help set bleeding colors. Note that a color that changes to soap may change back with an acid rinse; test it both ways.

Spot Cleaning

Cleaning spots only can be a problem because the soapy water or solvent will pick up the dirt and spread it out into a ring, resulting in a worse spot than the original. An additional difficulty: it is important not to rub or brush the silk as this may chafe it.

Use a series of soft cotton pads which have been soaked in the solvent then squeezed out. The more in excess the solvent, the more the ring will spread. Using a series of clean pads prevents dirty solvent from being left on the fabric. Dry pads placed under the spot will help absorb excess solvent. Work at the spot with a light padding motion.

When clean, gently feather out the wet spot. Work from the center of the cleaned area outwards to make a feathered sunburst with the edges imperceptibly blending into the untouched fabric *(Maher)*.

Dry Cleaning

Silk can be dry cleaned. It must be dry cleaned if there are colors not fast to soap washing, if it has an embossed or moiré design, if the dirt is oily or greasy, or if the material is heavily sized and you don't want the size removed. Hand-painted silks, if the paint is an oil base, cannot be dry cleaned as the fluid will solute the paint.

Dry cleaning is probably best left to professionals. All the solvents that can be used are either extremely flammable or toxic through the skin and to breathe, or both. Fluids which can be used include carbon tetrachloride (recommended because it is not flammable), acetone (available at building supplies — very effective and very flammable), and lighter fluid (available at grocery stores; also flammable). Always work outside, away from any flame, and wear rubber gloves.

Professional dry cleaners use per-chlor-ethylene or a similar petroleum-based fluid. The chlor is locked into the compound so that it is not harmful to the silk. This solvent has a little more drying effect on silk than does a special solvent used by some cleaners that do a lot of old textile work. This solvent, also petroleum based, was perfected in 1921 by a man named Stoddard, for whom it is named. It has had all the sulphur removed, it evaporates quickly and it has been deodorized so it leaves no smell. But most important for silk is that it is less drying. Unfortunately it is not available for home use.

The sound of silk tearing:
* A hundred trees rent by a storm*
in a moment — gone!

Bleaching

Never use chlorine bleach on silk. It is very alkaline and will just eat up the fiber. Sulphur and sulphides from burning sulphur, sodium peroxide, hydrogen peroxide and potassium permanganate are used to bleach silk. A simple method for bleaching silk at home can be found in Appendix III.

White silk is naturally very white. But the whiteness does vary by origin of the silk and by how carefully it's been handled. Historically, Chinese silk has been considered the whitest, and it was in demand in Europe for this quality. It's also a relatively hard gum. To preserve the whiteness, several successive degumming baths are used in order that the silk not be contaminated by its own dissolved gum. Japanese silk is said not to be so white, but to have a softer, more easily re-moved gum. The United States has historically obtained most of its silk from Japan.

In currently available silk fabrics, Sari or Indian silk is outstanding for its whiteness as well as its luster.

White silk noils, which are not a true white because of oils from the chrysalids, are sometimes bleached, although the fashion now is for "raw silk" natural noil fabric.

Bleached silk seems to take dye a little brighter and deeper than unbleached.

Some tussah (wild) silk is said to be bleachable, other not.

I have seen some tussah bleached to a true white, but most comes out a light off-white, usually a cool silvery-gray beige. Tussah is bleached so it can be dyed lighter, brighter colors than would be possible on a darker beige base.

Some sources report tussah to be difficult to dye unless it has been bleached (or even after bleaching), but I have found no problem. It dyes approximately the same dark colors, using the same amount of dye, as white silk. Light colors are muted by the natural beige base. It could be there are some other kinds of "tussah" wild silk which are more difficult to dye than those currently marketed.

Weighting

The weighting of silk is a wholly objectionable practice. Fortunately it is hardly, if at all, done anymore. But many beautiful semi-antique silks have disintegrated into dust because of the practice in the relatively near past.

Weighting of silk means the artificial addition of weight to pure silk fiber, beyond what is needed for dyeing colors. Dyed silk can be weighted with metal salts, especially iron, tin and lead, or with tannin or even sugar. Undyed silk may be

---

A family made a modest living by bleaching silk. They were able to do well because they used a secret salve, the recipe which had been handed down for generations. It kept their hands soft enough to handle the silk while they worked in water and chemicals.

One day a traveler learned of the salve and offered a huge sum of money for the formula.

After some debate they agreed to sell it to him.

He took the salve to the king, showed him its properties and was made a general in the army. Because the salve kept their hands from chapping, the archers were especially accurate and the army won all campaigns.

The family of silk bleachers, meanwhile, continued in their work.

Thus, each man uses his materials in his own way, and to his own ends.

Retold from Chuang tsu. See *Chuang Tsu*, translated by Burton Watson, Columbia University Press, New York, 1964.

---

weighted with lead, tin, sugar or with glue or gelatin sizings. It is the metal salts which are especially damaging to the silk. The other substances are deceptive, but they will wash out.

Black was almost invariably heavily weighted, sometimes by as much as 300%: a pound of silk was made to weigh four pounds! So filled with metal, the silk would crack and disintegrate, sometimes within a year's time.

It is unclear when the practice became common. It is not mentioned in 18th century dye books, but is (usually) railed against in late 19th century ones. By the early 20th century it was considered reprehensible by most of those in the silk trade, who could see the damage that was being done to the reputation and real value of silk.

However, there is evidence that these heavy silks were in great demand. In one book of ca. 1920, a silk fabric house describes how they imported some pure dye China silk, and no one believed it was silk because it was so light!

By law "pure dye" silk may have up to 10% by weight of non-silk in it; black may have 15%. Dyes are going to add some weight to the silk, there is no getting around it, but the greed of former silk dyers in weighting silk far beyond what was needed for color reproduction is inexcusable.

The effects of this bad practice are still being felt. Silk, the most durable of fibers, has gotten a reputation for "rotting" that is still not wholly forgotten.

Display and Storage

Heirloom silks should be carefully displayed and carefully stored. Intense light, heat and extremes of humidity are to be avoided. Also avoid any mountings which unduly strain certain threads, and folds, which may eventually become cracks.

Display silks in such a way that direct sunlight never falls upon them. Even as little as an hour a day adds up to many hours over a period of weeks, months, years. (Direct sunlight includes sunbeams through glass.) Intense artificial light, though it is not as strong as sunlight, adds up, too. Flourescents can be almost as destructive of colors as direct sunlight.

Choose walls and areas for display which are as far away as possible from sources of heat. On the other hand, a dank, dark corner is no place to show silk! The *tokonoma* of the traditional Japanese house provides a light, airy, but protected recess designed just for the appreciative display of such fragile treasures. Consider whether a slight rearrangement in your house could create such an area.

To store silks, wrap silk in silk: clean, white China silk — a treasure in a treasure. Special, non-acid forming tissue paper, Japanese "rice" paper, or well-washed unbleached muslin can also be used.

Where possible, roll silks rather than fold them. Where it is necessary to fold, add padding along the fold's inside so that it is actually a roll, not a crease. Creases eventually become cracks — in the same way you fold paper to more easily tear it.

Clean silks before storing. To remove dust, cover the silk with a screen and vacuum it gently, using the fabric-brush attachment.

Degumming Silk

Soap degumming is a process similar to scouring of wool: the raw silk is simmered in a soapy bath until the gum is dissolved, then the soapy solution is rinsed out. Here's how.

Weigh the raw silk. For each one-quarter pound of raw silk allow at least two gallons water and two ounces soap (three-quarters cup Ivory soap). Finer yarns/fabrics may need more room; wild silks may need more soap.

Begin with a lukewarm bath, add silk, bring to a simmer, and simmer *without boiling* until silk no longer feels slimy and looks lustrous and/or sparkly when pinched free of soap (this usually takes about 30 minutes). Rinse in successively cooler waters, ending with a little white vinegar (one-quarter cup) in the next to last rinse.

For extra-white silks and for tussahs, two degummings are done. The first is only partial, and a second degumming, called "boiling off", completes the process. Boiled-off liquor from white silk degumming may be saved and used during the dyeing of chemical colors, where it acts as a buffer against their harsh effects.

Caution: Most silk on the market is already degummed. Therefore, do not attempt to degum silk until you are sure it needs it. Do test a small portion if you are at all unsure.

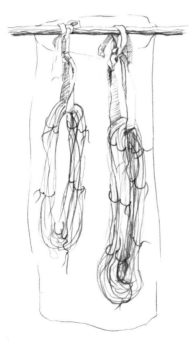

Yarn Handling

Wash and rinse yarns by holding them through the center of the skein and dipping up and down. Swishing and swirling yarn will only tangle it. Squeeze or wring out excess water, then shake out the yarn by holding it as for rinsing and gently shaking it. Work out tangles with the other hand or lay it

---

Scrope — Scroop — Scroup

Scroped silk is scrunchy, and rustles when touched.

To scrope silk, soak for ten to fifteen minutes in five percent white vinegar (acetic acid). Rinse and dry.

No one seems to know what causes scrope, only that the acid somehow affects the surface of the fiber. It seems to harden it, and scroped silk is not as soft as it was before scroping.

The process is reversible — washing in soap and water removes it.

---

down to pick apart bad ones. Change hand holds around the skein and shake and fuss until all tangles are out.

Then "snap" the skein. Snap it vigorously between two hands, palms facing. Or hang the skein from a hook or "arm" and snap by pulling sharply. (An "arm" is any smooth rod securely attached at one end. Someone's real arm will do, too.) If the skein is too big to effectively snap all at once, do it in sections. Change positions after each snap or two. If the yarn is weak and hasn't been well shaken, snapping may break strands, so work carefully at first.

The purpose of snapping is to straighten the strands of yarn and smooth down any loose fiber ends. Snapping takes kinks out of tightly twisted singles and smooths felted and matted yarns. Shaking and snapping also soften the yarn. Tussahs especially tend to dry very stiff unless shaken several times while drying.

"Slapping" is another method, very good for separating strands of matted singles or of sized yarns. With a simple overhand motion, slap the yarn down on a flat surface. Change holds around the skein as per usual and be firm but not overly vigorous. Slapping is done when the yarn is almost dry.

Further manipulations can be used to bring out more luster. Called variously "lustering" and "brightening", there are two basic procedures. One is twisting the skeins under pressure, sometimes with steam, the other involves stretching the yarn. Some interesting devices have been used for this: steam cabinets inside of which the yarn is stretched; multi-hooked "twisters"; heated rollers placed in series that both draw out and "iron" the yarn.

The simplest hand process is to "wring" the silk. It should be almost dry. Hold as for snapping, but instead, twist one hand around and around until the skein is wrung up as hard as possible. Shake out and repeat several times, changing positions each time. A "lustering hook" makes it easier as you can twist and pull at the same time. And a stick in the free loop makes a convenient handle. This wringing also rounds singles yarns, helps smooth felted yarns and softens yarns which have dried stiff.

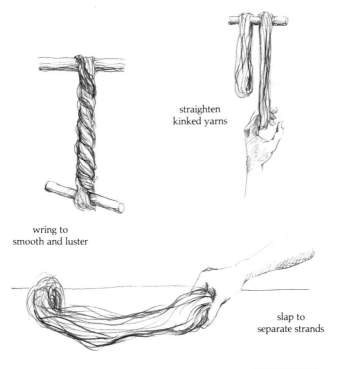

straighten
kinked yarns

wring to
smooth and luster

slap to
separate strands

The form of a short fibered spun silk yarn is amazingly variable. If it is handled carefully, snapped and lustered, then even after washing or dyeing it will retain its just-spun form. Sometimes it can even be made sleeker, denser and more lustrous. But, if it is squeezed a lot in washing/dyeing, and, if while drying, handling is minimal (just a little shaking to be sure the yarn doesn't dry stiff), it will be fluffy, light and lofty. A loose spun singles will show a lot of surface matting and increased sparkle; a tight spun singles will be kinky and extra-elastic.

Sizing

Sizing is an accessory to finishing and to weaving. Some fabrics need its strengthening effect or they will fray or fall apart. Sometimes the crispness it gives is wanted. Sometimes sizing is used to heighten sheen. Sizing is an important technique for the handweaver as sizing a warp makes it stronger, more elastic and less subject to fraying. By sizing a yarn, it is possible to take a short fibered, soft spun silk, barely strong enough for weft, and make it elastic and strong enough to use as warp.

Animal products are used for sizing silk, just as cellulose-like starch is used for cotton. The size in some ways approximates the original silk gum, except that it is transparent, shiny and water soluble, where silk gum is opaque, dull and does not wash out. The animal sizes are more elastic than starch; this is the main reason they're more appropriate to stretchy silk.

Gelatin and glue are the two main types. In commercial finishing gelatin is used for tightly woven fabrics and glue is used for sheer ones as it penetrates the fiber well and doesn't fill up the interstices of the weave. Heavy fabrics are given a diluted coating; thin fabrics, if they're wanted to be very stiff, get a thick coat. It can be sprayed on before ironing, or the whole fabric/garment can be dipped in the size after it is washed. If spraying, use a very fine spray to get the size spread as evenly as possible.

Brush sizing onto the back of velvet to more easily cut out odd shaped pieces for patchwork. Likewise, size loosely woven fabrics to obviate the need for stay stitching during garment construction. Sizing can be used to heighten sheen. It has its own refracting qualities and, as it helps smooth the surface of a textile, it increases the effect of silk's natural luster.

Sizing has been used on cheap manufactured silk fabrics to give them more body. This sizing is put on rather heavily, dried, then "broken" in a "tentering" machine that works like a European mangle: the fabric is repeatedly stretched on a slight bias. This breaks the glue between the yarns and softens the fabric so that it passes for a soft silk that feels more substantial than it really is. The practice isn't harmful to the fiber the way weighting is, but the fabric wears out more rapidly than expected, especially after the first washing takes all the size out.

A Silk Size

Size: mucilage glue, as it comes in the little bottles with rubber spreader-stoppers.

Proportions:

 2 tablespoons glue

 1 cup water

 ⅛ teaspoon white vinegar

For weaving warps, the easiest way to use this size is to apply it to the yarn in skeins before warping. Wet out the yarn directly in the size. Wring or squeeze out excess and hang to dry. While drying, shake, "snap" and "slap" (page 132) so that all strands separate.

The size can also be brushed onto the warp at the back of the loom, between back beam and heddles.

A larger proportion of water will give a lighter size, useful to smooth down a strong but "sticky" yarn.

To wash out the size: Soak for a few minutes in clear, cool water, then wash in Ivory soap and lukewarm water.

Appendix I

WEAVING NOTES

Weave dreams with
    silk
     gossamer fabrics
      fantastic beings
      landscapes of the soul
as delicate and
     luminous as
    the iris of your eyes
reflecting misted light.

Weaving with silk is truly the subject to fill another book. Here, though, are some handweaving notes.

Silk is warped according to its type, which may be fuzzy, fluffy, elastic, smooth, strong, slippery, fine or fat, etc. Techniques appropriate to wool are best for fuzzy, fluffy, elastic yarns; techniques appropriate to cotton or linen are best for the smooth, slippery kinds of yarns.

The smooth, strong, but less obviously elastic yarns should be beamed with a fair amount of tension. Fluffy, weak or very elastic yarns should be put on with as little tension as practical. Fine yarns are best warped sectionally. This prevents tangling; tangles in a fine silk can be impossible to pick apart.

Sett and beat silk tightly — as tightly as possible. While the fabric will be very stiff when it comes off the loom, it will quickly soften. If the sett and beat are too open, the fabric will soften too much and become sleazy. Of course, weave purely visual fabrics such as casements as openly as desired.

Gait the loom with care: check all adjustments so that sheds are small and clean. Always release tension on the warp when not weaving.

Increase the moisture in the room to prevent "fly-away" ends in threading and "snap back" of the weft in picking due to electrostaticity.

Beat once, firmly, just when changing sheds.

Weave silk off reasonably quickly to preserve its elasticity.

Allow time for breaking in the fabric: a softening up period.

Always use the finest materials available to you. And be bold in trying out your own ideas, designs and weaves, even if this be but a slight modification to an existing pattern. Your time — your life — is your most precious gift, and each of us is unique. Your weaving is meant as the flower of this uniqueness.

Weaves

I am often asked, "How can I weave a soft silk — my silks are so stiff!" When questioned, I always explain that these fabrics are invariably done in plain weave. Plain weave is the simplest but also the most unyielding weave there is. Structurally, the yarns must bend the most: every yarn bends every time it crosses every other yarn. Even a simple twill cuts those bends by 50%. These plain weaves will eventually wear soft as the fiber molds into its new wavy position. But this takes time, and weavers often don't want to wait.

The following ways to construct a firmly woven but open and soft fabric might be explored:

Gauze crossings to hold the threads in place.

Bands of tightly woven areas interspersed with more openly *sett* and/or beat areas such as Mock Leno, or interspersed with open *weave* areas such as huckaback, huck-lace, Bronson spot, honeycomb, basket weave, etc.

Areas of open weave securely "tied" together using such techniques as Spanish lace, Brook's Bouquet, hemstitching or gauze crossings.

Thick and thin yarns arranged to form areas of tight plain weave (thick yarns or slubs crossing) and areas of open plain weave (thin yarns crossing).

Basic weaves other than plain weave to explore: twills, especially undulating twills, and satins.

Looms

Silk can be woven on any loom; however, if you have a choice, these features are preferred:

Counterbalance or countermarche, for the even shed tension these systems provide. Also, because they are balanced, they are less work to weave on.

A weighted back beam. This puts the least strain on the warp, as the tension on the warp is always the same no matter what position the shed, nor how close to the beater the weaving has crept.

An overhead beater. Because of the arc of swing, an overhead beater will not chafe the warp during beat-up. A floor-pivot beater should be provided with a very smooth shuttle race to prevent the warp from being badly chafed by the reed's lower edge.

A long warp—a deep loom. The longer the warp from heddles to back beam, the less strain is placed on it in the weaving operations.

"L'art de la décoration des étoffes de soie est de tous les arts celui peut-être qui permet le mieux de suivre les évolutions de l'ornement dont il constitue en quelque sorte la synthèse. Plus que tout autre il reflète l'esprite des temps, étant par excellence art intime et utile. Chaque race y laisse l'empreinte de son génie, chaque civilisation la trace de ses efforts et de ses aspirations."
— Raymond Cox in "Les Soieries D'Art"

"The art of the decoration of fabrics of silk is, perhaps, of all the arts, that which permits the best study of the evolution of ornament. For it constitutes a kind of synthesis: more than any other, it reflects the spirit of the times, because it is an art both personal and functional. There, each race leaves the imprint of its genius, each civilization records its efforts and aspirations."

Appendix II
KNITTING NOTES

compiled by Joan Schrouder, knitting consultant

Any silk yarn can be knit. However, for the effect you want, choose carefully and *always make a swatch,* or two. Swatches should be made 4″ to 6″ square. Measure the entire finished swatch, then wash, dry and finish exactly as you would the projected piece. *Now* check the gauge. Pull and stretch the sample swatch, and remeasure to estimate stretchiness in both length and width.

Stretch

Silk knits have a tendency to stretch. Most of this tendency is due to the slipperiness of the fiber. So, unless a lacy effect is wanted, knit a little tighter than you think you should. Tight knitting stretches less than loose knitting. And generally, fluffy spun silk yarns stretch less than smooth spun. Five percent is a minimum stretch expectation, so for a sweater adapted from a wool recipe, knit to a size smaller.

A helpful technique to minimize stretching is to knit or purl into the *backs* of the stitches, thereby twisting them. Don't hesitate to try out cables or other pattern stitches that tend to pull in or tighten the knit. Avoid lace pattern areas unless the whole piece is knit lacy, for the lace pattern areas are likely to stretch more than the plain knit areas. This differential can be used to nice effect, if controlled. Cuffs, necks and welts may need elastic thread sewn in.

Until you are familiar with how your chosen silk yarn or yarns handle, choose a style of garment where a little stretch won't detract from the end result. For instance: raglan or drop-shoulder sleeves; tunic-length or bloused sweater instead of fitted waist; or flowing skirt rather than fitted.

With set-in sleeves, knit 1″ narrower than body measure on the shoulders for short sleeves, 2″ narrower for long sleeves. The pull of the sleeves will widen the shoulders out.

Knit sweaters from the top down, so length can be checked as you knit. Also, alterations are then easier, in case the silk stretches more or less than expected. Note that singles yarns have a tendency to stretch on the diagonal, so a plied silk is a better choice for most knitting.

Cleaning

Dry clean only if necessary because of colors. Otherwise, hand wash and lay flat to dry. This tends to restore the original size of the garment in case it has stretched on wearing. When washing, support the whole of the wet piece, so the weight of the water doesn't pull on it. A layer of cheesecloth on the bottom of the wash tub can be lifted by its four corners to transfer the silk knit to rinse water. (For general wash instructions for silk see page 117.) The least handling is best: let the silk drip drain in a collander, still in the cheesecloth, for 15 to 30 minutes. Then, on a towel on a flat surface, spread out the cheesecloth and gently shape out the silk knit.

For fluffy tussahs a machine dryer can be used at this point, as suggested for very sturdy handwoven silks on page 117. Use caution: only a very few silk knits will benefit from this; try it out on the swatch first.

A small "travel style" hand steamer is a great tool to fluff out and relax the silk once it is dry. Another method, recommended by Susan Druding of Crystal Palace Yarns in *Silk, Silk, Silk*, is to steam iron through a thick bath towel *without using any pressure* on the silk.

Some manipulation may be needed, especially with tussahs, to soften the fiber after it's washed. Simply roll the piece up in a thin towel, rather tightly, unroll, and roll again in each of the four directions. Repeat if necessary; in stubbornly stiff cases, steam a little first. Silk that dries very stiff may not have been rinsed enough. (Remember to add a little white vinegar in the next to last rinse water.) Dry cleaning obviates this stiffness, so stubbornly stiff silks may better be dry cleaned.

Storage

Store silk knits as flat as possible. For instance, use an entire dresser drawer just for knits, and lay them out the full

To estimate gauge where suggested weaving sett or "ends-per-inch" is known, divide the suggested sett by two to get the approximate stitches per inch.

An estimate guide for amounts of silk yarn needed for a size 40 sweater:

- A "sport weight" size yarn that gauges at 6 stitches to the inch in stockinette needs about 1400 to 1600 yards. (About 12 to 14 ounces of a smooth spun 8/2 m.c. at 1920 yd/lb.)
- A "knitting worsted" size yarn that gauges 5 stitches to the inch needs about 1000 to 1200 yards. (About 12 ounces of a soft spun 8/2, or a soft spun 7/2 at 1550 yd/lb.)
- A "semi-bulky" at 4 stitches per inch needs about 800 to 1000 yards.
- A true "bulky" size yarn at 3 stitches to the inch needs about 700 to 800 yards. (About one pound of very heavy 3.5/2 m.c. silk.)
- Lace takes maybe ⅔ these amounts.
- Cable knits take maybe ⅓ more.

size of the drawer. Separate each piece with a layer of tissue or old sheeting, and completely lift off the overlaying pieces to remove one below. Or, fold the silk knits loosely and arrange only one layer deep. Never hang silk knits on hangers, as this will pull the shoulders badly, but an arrangement where they are draped over thick dowel or tubes is possible.

Thinner knits can also be stored rolled on tubes. Cover the silk with tissue or sheeting, then roll on a thick tube, being careful no creases develop. The sheeting can be cinched with rubber bands or ties beyond the extent of the silk and the tube stored vertically for convenience.

Appendix III

HOME BLEACHING OF SILK

- Hydrogen peroxide (H_2O_2), 3% solution, as available in drugstores and supermarkets.
- Wet out the silk in warm water.
- Cover, with enough room to move the silk about, in a solution of warm water and hydrogen peroxide.
- Amounts needed vary with type of silk, spin and degree of bleaching desired. Estimates: 1 pint hydrogen peroxide for 1 pound white silk or natural white silk noil (bleaching an off-white to a white); 4 pints (2 quarts) hydrogen peroxide for 1 pound tussah silk (bleaching a beige to creamy white). Plus water to cover, with room to turn and gently move the silk about.
- Heat slowly; turn silk occasionally. Simmer (not boil) about an hour. If not light enough, lift out silk, add more hydrogen peroxide, and repeat. Cool, rinse and dry. See pages 131-133 for handling while drying.
- Luster is undiminished; both strength and weight are unchanged. This bleached white has a soft pearly-creamy quality. It is not as stark as most commercially bleached whites. It is the perfection of "wedding dress white".

SUPPLIERS BY MAIL

Silk Fiber for Spinning

Jean Case, Fallbrook House
R.D.2, Box 17
Troy, Pennsylvania 16947

Straw Into Gold,
Crystal Palace Yarns
3006 San Pablo Avenue
Berkeley, California 94702

Forté Fibers
P.O. Box 818
Palisade, Colorado 81526

The Fiber Studio
Foster Hill Road
Henniker, New Hampshire 03242

**Silk Yarns for Weaving,
Knitting and Crochet**
(• *denotes hand dyed colors*)

Cheryl Kolander-Williams
Aurora Silk•
5806 North Vancouver Avenue
Portland, Oregon 97217

Crystal Palace Yarns•
3006 San Pablo Avenue
Berkeley, California 94702

The Fiber Studio
Foster Hill Road
Henniker, New Hampshire 03242

Robin and Russ Handweavers
533 North Adams
McMinnville, Oregon 97128

The Silk Tree
26727 Ferguson Avenue
Whonnock, British Columbia
Canada V0M 1S0

The Drop Spindle•
417 E. Central
Santa Maria, California 93454

Nancy, Custom Handweaving
Box 477
Redondo Beach, California 90277

Dyeworks•
2750 Nicollet Square
Minneapolis, Minnesota 55408

Kreinik Manufacturing Co.
P.O. Box 1966
Parkersburg, West Virginia 26101

Robert Joseph Co.
2533 Gilbert Avenue
Cincinnati, Ohio 45206

Embroidery Threads

The Needlework Shop
Royal Ridge Mall
Nashua, New Hampshire

Craft Gallery and Stitchery, Ltd.
96 South Broadway
South Nyack, New York

Cheryl Kolander-Williams
Aurora Silk
5806 North Vancouver Avenue
Portland, Oregon 97217
(hand dyed, natural dyed colors)

The Needlecraft Shop
P.O. Box 2147
Canoga Park, California 91306

Kirsten Barrere
J.L. Walsh Silks
4338 Edgewood
Oakland, California 94602
(hand dyed)

Fabrics

Thai Silks
252 State Street
Los Altos, California 94022

Kasuri Dyeworks
1959 Shattuck Avenue
Berkeley, California

Cerulean Blue
P.O. Box 21168
Seattle, Washington 98111

BIBLIOGRAPHY

Baity, Elizabeth Chesley. *Man is a Weaver*. New York: The Viking Press, 1942.

Bath, Virginia Churchill. Embroidery Masterworks from the Textile Collection of the Art Institute of Chicago. Chicago: Henry Regnery Co., 1972.

Belding, Hemmingway Co. *A Story: The Gift of the Silk Worm*. 1930.

Bell, Quentin. *On Human Finery*. 2nd edition. New York: Schocken, 1976. (The *why* of fashion.)

Boulnois, Luce. *The Silk Road*. New York: E.P. Dutton and Co., 1966. Translated by Dennis Chamberlain from the French: *La Route de la Soie*, Paris: Arthaud, 1963. (History, following a thread of silk.)

Bunt, Cyril G.E. *The Silks of Lyons and Philippe de Lasalle*. Leigh-on-Sea, England: F. Lewis Publishers, Ltd., 1960. (One of a series, "The World's Heritage of Woven Fabrics" under the general editorship of Cyril Bunt.)

Calico Museum of Textiles. *Journal of Indian Textile History*, number VII. Ahmedabad, India: Calico Museum of Textiles, 1967. (An article by Pupul Jayakar on the Naksha Bandhas of Banares details the making of the portable drawloom simples [pattern harps] used for the patterning of elaborate silk brocades.)

Central Raw Silk Association of Japan. *A Story of Raw Silk*. From the Golden Gate Exposition, San Francisco, 1939.

Chinatex promotional brochures, including *Spring Flowers Blossom on Silk, Chinese Pure Silk Fabrics, Silk Yarn Catalog* and *Chinese Silk Fabrics*.

Cole, Alan S. *Ornament in European Silks*. London: Debenham and Freebody, 1899. (A classic.)

Cooper, Beowulf A., ed. *A Silkmoth Rearer's Handbook*. London: The Amateur Entomologist's Society, 1956. (This is volume 12 of "The Amateur Entomologist", rewritten, re-illustrated and expanded by W.J.B. Crotch. Raising wild silkworms; includes catalog of wild silk moths of the world.)

Cooper, Elizabeth K. *Silkworms and Science, The Story of Silk*. New York: Harcourt, Brace & World Inc., 1961. (Good primer.)

Corticelli Silk Co. *Silk; It's Origin, Culture and Manufacture*. 1919 and later editions. (Photos of silk culture and reeling in Japan.)

Cox, Raymond. *Les Soieries d'Art depuis les Origines Jusqu'à nos Jours*. Paris: Librairie Hachette, 1914. (Raymond Cox was the director of the Musée Historique des Tissus de la Chambre de Commerce de Lyon, and this work is a classic cited in the bibliographies of all major works which follow it. As far as I know there is no English translation. If you have read Boulnois' *Silk Road* you will understand that the Continental view of history and design is different from the English. I would like to prepare a translation.)

Crockett, Candace. *The Complete Spinning Book*. New York: Watson-Guptill, 1977. (Has a section on raising and hand-reeling silk.)

Darby, W.D. *Silk, the Queen of Fabrics*. New York: Dry Goods Economist, 1922. (A look at the silk industry in America of the 1920s.)

Davenport, Elsie G. *Your Handspinning*. Mountain View, Missouri: Select Books, 1964.

Davison, Marguerite Porter. *A Handweaver's Pattern Book.* Swarthmore, Pennsylvania: Marguerite Porter Davison, revised edition 1950.

Duran, Leo. *Raw Silk, A Practical Handbook for the Buyer.* New York: Silk Publishing Co., 1913 and later editions. (A history of silk reeling.)

The Encyclopedia Britannica. *A Dictionary of Arts, Sciences, Literature and General Information,* 11th Edition. New York: The Encyclopedia Britannica Co., 1910.

Errera, Isabelle. *Catalogue D'Étoffes Ancienne et Modernes.* 3rd Edition. Bruxelles: Musées Royaux du Cinquantenaire, Vromant & Co., 1927.

Fessenden, Thomas G. *The New American Gardener: containing practical directions on the culture of fruits and vegetables; including landscape and ornamental gardening, grape-vines, silk, strawberries, etc.* 4th Edition. Boston: Carter and Hendee, 1830. (A classic. The 14 pages on silk begin: "All hail, Agriculture and its noble bands! . . . There, since the days of old, has been the firm foundation of national greatness and prosperity; and there it must remain until the end of time.")

Flemming, Ernst. *An Encyclopaedia of Textiles, from the earliest times to the beginning of the 19th century.* Berlin: Ernst Wasmuth Ltd., 1927.

-----. *Encyclopaedia of Textiles, completely revised by Renate Jaques.* London: A. Zwemmer Ltd., 1958.

Gaddum, H.T. *Silk, How and Where it is Produced.* Macclesfield, England: H.T. Gaddum & Co. Ltd., 1948 and later.

Harris, Christie and Moira Johnston. *Figleafing Through History: The dynamics of dress.* New York: Atheneum, 1971. (Discusses the *meaning* of dress changes through the ages.)

Hayashi, Ryoichi. *The Silk Road and the Shoso-in.* New York/Tokyo: Weatherhill/Heibonsha, 1975. (Translated by Robert Ricketts from *Shiruku Rodo to Shoso-in.* Volume 6 of the Heibonsha Survey of Japanese Art. Discusses the eastern end of the Silk Road (in Japan), and articles, including textiles, which moved eastwards and have been preserved in the Shoso-in and other repositories in Japan.)

Hochberg, Bette. *Handspinner's Handbook.* Santa Cruz, California: Bette Hochberg, 1976.

Hooper, Luther. *Silk: Its Production and Manufacture.* London: Sir Isaac Pitman and Sons, Ltd., n.d., but before 1917. (Includes a discussion of drawloom silk weaving, later expanded into his *Handloom Weaving, Plain and Ornamental.)*

Howitt, F.O. *Bibliography of the Technical Literature on Silk.* New York: Hutchinson's Scientific and Technical Publications, 1946. (Discusses research published in magazine articles and books.)

Huber, Charles J. in Mathews' *The Textile Fibres* (q.v.). (Huber wrote the silk section in later edition.)

Hummel, J.J. *Textile Fabrics and Their Preparation for Dyeing.* London: Cassell and Company, revised edition 1906.

Hurst, George H. *Silk Dyeing, Printing and Finishing.* New York: George Bell and Sons, 1892.

Japan's Ministry of Agriculture and Forestry, International Cooperation Section. *Handbook of Silkworm Rearing, Agriculture Technique Manual 1.* Tokyo: Fugi Publishing Co., 1972. (All aspects of modern silkworm rearing, including mulberry cultivation. Thorough and technical; recommended for serious silk raisers.)

Jaques, Renate. (See Flemming).

Kendrick, A.F. *Catalogue of Early Medieval Woven Fabrics*. London: Victoria and Albert Museum, Department of Textiles, 1925.

Lane, Rose Wilder. *Woman's Day Book of American Needlework*. New York: Simon & Schuster, 1963. (A number of the illustrations are 17th and 18th century American silks.)

Lister, Margot. *Costume, An Illustrated Survey from Ancient Times to the 20th Century*. Boston: Plays, Inc., ca. 1972.

Lutz, Frank E. *Field Book of Insects*, 3rd edition. New York: G.P. Putnam's Sons, 1948. ("A Putnam Nature Field Book", original edition, 1918. Best identification of North American wild silkmoths, caterpillars and cocoons.)

Maher, Jeannie W. *Silk Finishing*. Maryland: National Institute of Cleaning and Dyeing, 1938. (Reissued in 1943. Ironing and sizing of silk garments.)

Manchester, H.H. *The Story of Silk and Cheney Silks*. South Manchester, Connecticut: Cheney Brothers, 1916, revised 1924.

Margolis, Adele P. *The Complete Book of Tailoring — For Women Who Like To Sew*. Garden City, New York: Doubleday & Co., Inc., 1964. (I *hate* to sew, and this is still the best sewing book around. Includes, for instance, four different ways to make a bound buttonhole, in extra heavy fabrics to sheers.)

Mathews, J. Merritt. *The Textile Fibers, Their Physical, Microscopical and Chemical Properties*. New York: John Wiley and Sons, 1904 and later editions.

May, Florence Lewis. *Silk Textiles of Spain, Eighth to Fifteenth Century*. New York: The Hispanic Society of America, 1957.

Minnich, Helen Benton. *Japanese Costume and the Makers of Its Elegant Tradition*. In collaboration with Shojiro Nomura. Rutland, Vermont: Charles E. Tuttle Co., 1963. (A beautifully written book based on the researches of Japanese textile historians into their rich but vanishing past. Mr. Nomura is most famous for assembling — in many cases reconstructing — a large collection of classic Kimono.)

Museum of the Sinkiang-Uighur Autonomous Region and The Group in Charge of the Exhibition of Cultural Relics, editors. *The Silk Road, Fabrics from the Han to the T'ang Dynasty*. The People's Republic of China, 1973. (In Chinese, with translation of the introduction by *China Books and Periodicals*, New York. Textiles recently unearthed from graves along the ancient silk route. Life-size color prints so well done you can almost feel them. A standard for textile reproduction.)

Noma, Seiroku. *Japanese Costume and Textile Arts*. New York/Tokyo: Weatherhill/Heibonsha, 1973. (Translated by Armins Nikovskis from *Kosode to No-isho*. Vol. 16 of the Heibonsha Survey of Japanese Art.)

Oelsner, G.H. *A Handbook of Weaves*. Dover, New York: Macmillan, 1915, reprinted 1952. (Translated by Samuel S. Dale.)

Secretary of the Treasury. *Growth and Manufacture of Silk, Adapted to the Different Parts of the Union*. To the Committee on Agriculture of the House of Representatives, 20th Congress, 1st Session. Washington, 1818. (A 220-page "letter" reporting on all aspects of silk with an eye to encouraging sericulture in the U.S.)

Shimmin, Marguerite. *Silkworms and Silk*. Pasadena, California: Gravender Spinners and Marguerite Shimmin, n.d. (A folder on raising silk.)

Silk and Rayon Users Association, Inc. *The Silk Book*. London: The Silk and Rayon Users Association, Inc., 1951.

Simmons, Pauline. *Chinese Patterned Silks*. New York: The Metropolitan Museum of Art, 1948.

Slomann, Vilhelm. *Bizarre Designs in Silks, Trade and Traditions*. Copenhagen: Ejnar Munksgaard, 1953 (for the New York Carlsberg Foundation).

Thompson, Eliza B. *Silk (The Silk Department, Department Store Merchandise Manuals)*. New York: The Ronald Press Co., 1918.

Tuchscherer, Jean-Michel and Gabriel Vial. *Le Musée Historique des Tissus de Lyon*. Lyon: Albert Guillot, 1977. (Sixty-two photos of their collection of historic silks plus some photos of a reconstructed loom of the type used by Phillipe de Lasalle; a fascinating contraption of sticks and string.)

Watson, William. *Textile Design and Colour, Elementary Weaves and Figured Fabrics*. 5th Edition. New York: Longmans Green and Co., 1946. (Classic industrial weaving text, compliments his *Advanced Textile Design*, (first edition, 1912) which discusses advanced weaves such as damask, gauze and velvet.)

Wheeler, Monroe, ed. *Textiles and Ornaments of India*. New York: The Museum of Modern Art, 1956. (Texts by Pupul Jayakar and John Irwin. Based on an exhibition held in 1955.)

Wieger, Dr. L.S.J. *Chinese Characters: their origin, etymology, history, classification and signification. A thorough study from Chinese documents*. New York: Paragon Book Reprint Corp. and Dover Publications, Inc. 1965. (Translated from the second French edition of 1927 by L. Davrout, S.J. The first edition was published in 1915.)

Wilcox, R. Turner. *The Dictionary of Costume*. New York: Charles Scribner's Sons, 1969.

Williams, Carrie. *Rearing Silkworms*. San Francisco: The Whitaker and Ray Co., 1902. (Ms. Williams raised silkworms in the San Diego area.)

Wolfensberger, Arnold. *Theory of Silk Weaving*. New York: The American Silk Journal Co., 1896. (Drafts of basic silk fabrics for the industry of the time.)

Volavková, Hana. *The Synagogue Treasures of Bohemia and Moravia*. Translated by G. Hort and Roberta Finlayson Samsour. Published by SFINX, Prague, 1949 in cooperation with the Jewish Museum, Prague.

Volbach, W. Fritz. *Early Decorative Textiles*. New York: Paul Hamlyn, 1969. (Translated by Yuri Gabriel from the Italian *Il Tessuto Nell'arte Antica*, Milan, 1966. Sassano-Byzantine silks and Coptic wools in color.)

GLOSSARY: TERMS OF THE TRADE

Art Silk, Artificial Silk. Rayon.

Bave. The double silk filament as spun by the silkworm.

Boiling-Off. Degumming of raw silk by boiling in soapy water, especially the finishing soap bath if more than one is used.

Book. A bundle of raw silk skeins. Japanese books weigh about 4-4½ pounds and contain about 50-60 skeins. Chinese books are heavier.

Bourré (Fr.). Raw silk waste.

Brightening. Oiling the silk with an emulsion of olive oil and washing soda, then scroping.

Brin. A single silk filament. Two brins cemented together by silk gum make one bave, the double filament as spun by the silkworm.

Byssus. Sea silk or pinna. A silk-like fiber secreted by a shellfish, *Pinna nobilis,* and related species. The short (4-6cm) fibers can be spun, and a small industry in southern Italy at one time made gloves and stockings of it. Said to be very soft and warm and of glossy brown or gold color. *(Huber, in Mathews)*

Calendering. A pressing of fabric between heavy rollers, usually with heat and sometimes steam, to give a very smooth finish. Done especially to satins.

Ciré (Fr.). A finish that gives a very shiny surface. It is a waxy coating used especially on satins and black silks and is sometimes printed to make floral designs.

Conditioning, Conditioned Silk. Silk is so absorbtive of moisture that in order to get an accurate weight on a lot of raw silk, a sample is "conditioned". First it is weighed "as is", then it is dried in an oven until all the moisture is out, at which time it is weighed again. 11% of the bone-dry weight is added to represent a normal amount of moisture that silk can be expected to have. This conditioned weight is compared to the first, actual weight, then the conditioned weight of the whole lot can be computed.

Count. The number given a yarn to indicate its yardage per weight. There are three main systems: deniers for reeled silk yarns; metric for spun silks; and English for English-spun silks. *See also* Dram.

Deniers (Fr.). *See* Count.

Discharging. Degumming.

Dobby. A device attached to a loom which automatically controls the shedding of harnesses, as distinct from the Jacquard which controls individual heddles.

Doup. A special loop heddle used for automatic shedding of gauze. Also used as abbreviation for doupionni.

Doupionni. *(Various spellings, Fr., It.)* A raw silk reeled from double cocoons.

Dram. English system for thrown silk, the equivalent of the denier. A dram is ¹⁄₁₆ of an ounce. The system is based on 1000 yards to the dram, or 256,000 yards to the pound for size number 1. Dividing 256,000 by any dramage gives the yardage per pound.

Dynamited Silk. Silk very heavily weighted with tin salts.

Ecru Silk (Fr.) Thrown silk either fully raw or with only a small amount of the gum removed.

Extra-Luster. Heightened sheen on skein silk from being stretched while steamed.

Fibroin. The silk fiber. Raw silk is made up of fibroin, the core fiber, with a coat of sericin or silk gum.

Filature. A silk reeling house.

Filling. Weft.

Finishing. Any treatment given to a fabric after weaving and to garments after cleaning to improve appearance and hand. For instance, washing, felting, sizing, ironing (but not applied to the cleaning of soil).

Floss. The loose silk that is first spun by the silkworm: it makes a sort of hammock for the cocoon. Also, a soft silk yarn of almost no twist used especially for embroidery.

Frison (Fr.). Silk waste from the reeling process, especially the outer waste (floss).

Gassing. Singeing off the hairiness of a yarn or fabric.

Grège (Fr.). Raw silk as it comes from the filature.

Grey Goods. Fabric to be, but not yet, piece degummed and dyed.

Gum Silk. Thrown raw silk.

Gut. The filament obtained by slitting open a mature silkworm, removing the silk glands and stretching them out to about a half-yard length. Transparent in water, it is used for fishing lead lines and for surgical sutures.

Hand. Feel, including body, drape and touch (surface).

Hank. Of silk is 120 yards.

Hard Silk. Thrown raw silk.

Kapok. Silk cotton tree. Fibers 1" long, silky in feel, used for stuffing.

Knubs. Frison (q.v.).

Ligne. $\frac{1}{12}$th of a French inch, equals .0883 of an English inch; used for measuring ribbon widths.

Loading. Weighting or other adulteration of silk.

Lousy Silk. Silk that on weaving shows light colored specks on the surface of the fabric due to the filaments splitting in fibrils, curling up and forming small neps.

Lustering. The silk is stretched then ironed between rollers or steamed to set the fibers parallel. Used after dyeing or washing to increase luster of yarn or fabric.

Machine Twist. Thread designed for use on sewing machines.

M.C. Metric count. *See* Count.

Metallic Dye. Extra-luster (q.v.).

Miscuit (Fr: half-done). Silk dyed in about a half degummed state.

Momme. "A Japanese weight equal to 3.75 grams which is applied to a piece of fabric measuring 25 yards by 1.49 inches, an area of 1.035 square yards: thus a 1-momme silk weighs 3.62 grams per square yard." *(Howwitt).* Or, an 8-momme silk would weigh about 1 ounce per square yard. Habutai, for instance, is woven from 2.5 to 60 momme, with the China Silk class commonly in the 8 to 14 momme range. Abbreviated as mm.

Nep, Nepp, Nib, Nubb, etc. Small bits of fiber that stick above the surface of an otherwise smooth silk yarn or fabric.

Nett Silk. Reeled silk.

Organzine. Silk yarn for warp: two or more raw singles which have been tightly twisted in one direction, are put together and tightly twisted in the other direction.

Pari (Fr.). The weight of raw silk before boiling-off. Par Weighting is weighting that returns the degummed silk to its pari (raw) weight.

Piece. A length of goods. Broadsilks usually 60 yards, ribbons 10 yards.

Piece-Dyeing, Piece-Dyed. Fabric dyed after weaving.

Pierced Cocoons. Cocoons from which the moth has emerged.

Polishing. A finish to fabric that heightens its luster.

Pure-Dye. Dyed but unweighted silk.

Raw Goods. Fabrics for piece dyeing.

Raw Silk. Silk as it comes from the cocoons, with all its gum.

Regain. The standard amount of moisture to be added to a completely dried out fiber to bring it to conditioned weight, 11% in the case of silk.

Ribbon, Riband, Ribband. A narrow fabric of silk, technically under 18″ wide, usually under 12″.

Sericin. The outer coating of silk gum on the raw silk fiber, soluble in hot soapy water.

Showerproof, Rainproof. Fabric treated so it does not spot by water.

Skein. A coil of yarn, also called a hank. Usually 45″-54″ in circumference.

Skein-dyed. Dyed in skein form before weaving.

Slubs, Slugs. Soft thick lumps in a yarn.

Soft Silk. Thrown silk yarn, degummed, dyed or not.

Soie (Fr.). Silk.

Souple Silk. Skein-dyed silk with only a small portion of the gum removed. Firmer but less lustrous than fully degummed.

Steam Silk. Filature reeled as opposed to hand reeled.

Steam Stretched. Skeins given an extra luster by being stretched while steamed.

Stripping. Degumming.

Tender Goods. Fabrics not strong enough for use due to being damaged by, for instance, improper dyeing.

Throwing. Twisting reeled raw silk into yarn.

Throwster. One who throws silk.

Thrums. The ends of a warp which, due to the mechanics of most looms, cannot be woven. Usually about one yard long.

Tram. Raw silk threads, slightly twisted, for weft.

Traverse. A to-and-fro motion used to wind yarn into a skein or onto a bobbin in a criss-cross manner. This makes it easier to find a broken end in unwinding.

Twist Silk. Sewing silk.

Vegetable Silk. A number of plant seeds have downy coats, silky in feel. Kapok (q.v.) is the most commercially valuable.

Waste. Any unreelable silk. The raw material for spun silks.

Waterproof. Treated to be impervious to water. Silk is said to be waterproofed by being dipped in boiled linseed oil and dried.

INDEX

macramé, 81 (Plate XI)
map, frontispiece
manufacture, 6, 29-37
mawata, silk squares, 72
Mexico, 5, 41 (Plate III)
microscope, 28
mulberry, 3, 17
noil, 47, 48, 54-56, 58, 65, 76-78, 103
organzine, 30, 60
paper, 42 (Plate IV), 104
Persia, 3, 106
Phillipe de LaSalle, 5, 89, 99
pile fabrics and carpets, 12, 20, 40 (Plate II), 66, 86 (Plate XVI), 113, 114, 122
ply, 57, 61-62, 63, 66
raising silk, *see* sericulture
raw silk, 14, 16, 17-20, 29-34, 55, 71, 105 *see also* noil
reeling, reeled silk, 17-18, 29-37, 52-53, 55, 58, 60, 67, 72, 74, 78
reprocessed silk, 54, 56, 58
resiliency, 13, 26 *see also* hand
Rome, 2
"rot", 14, 128-129
Russia, 8
schapping, 15, 16
scrope, 49, 132
sericulture, 1-8, 17-19, 24
setting the twist, 77
sewing, 67
shrinkage, 123-124
silk gum, 25 *see also* raw silk *and* degumming
silk moths, 21-23
Silk Road, 2, frontispiece
silk worms, 21-23
sizing, 49, 116, 134, 135 *see also* counts
soap, 116
storage, 130
strength, 12, 50-51, 54, 59, 61-66
spider silk, 18

spun silk, 19-20, 29-67 *see also* handspinning
tables *see* glossaries
tapestry, 3, 85 (Plate XV), 100
thrown silk *see* reeling
tie-dye, 8
tram, 30, 42 (Plate IV)
tussah, 19-21, 24, 29, 36, 37, 40 (Plate II), 51, 55, 66, 72-77, 105, 106, 112, 127-128, 130 *see also* wild silk
United States, 5, 6, 8, 40 (Plate II), 42 (Plate IV), 81 (Plate XI), 83 (Plate XIII), 84 (Plate XIV), 86 (Plate XVI)
velvet *see* pile fabrics
warmth, 10-11, 26
warp, 13, 30, 50, 51, 54, 55, 59, 137, 138
washing, 115-120, 124, 125, 126
weft, 30, 50, 54, 138
weighting, 14, 128-129
wild silks, 5, 19-23, 24, 28, 41 (Plate III), 48 *see also* tussah
yarns, 29-67, 131-133, 137-139